Positive Attitudes for the 50+ Years

How Anyone Can Make Them Happy & Fulfilling

by

Willard A. Scofield

MAGNUS PRESS

MAGNUS PRESS

P.O. Box 2666
Carlsbad, CA 92018

Positive Attitudes for the 50+ Years:
How Anyone Can Make Them Happy & Fulfilling

Copyright ©1998 Willard A. Scofield

First Edition, 1998

Printed in the United States of America

ISBN 0-9654806-2-3

Publisher's Cataloging-in-Publication
(Provided by Quality Books, Inc.)

Scofield, Willard Arthur.
     Positive attitudes for the 50+ years: how anyone can make them
     happy and fulfilling / by Willard A. Scofield.

     p. cm.
     Includes index.
     Preassigned LCCN: 98-67443
     ISBN: 0-9654806-2-3

     1. Aging—Religious aspects—Christianity. 2. Happiness in old age.
     3. Attitude (Psychology) I. Title. II. Title: Positive attitudes for
     the fifty-plus years

BV4580.S36 1998   248.8'5
                                                   QBI98-1123

---

02 01 00 99 98   10 9 8 7 6 5 4 3 2 1

To Norma with thanks for
forty-four years of happy marriage

Contents

Introduction

Is it possible to believe that the senior years may be the happiest and most fulfilling of our lives?

This book says that we can believe just that. Instead of doors slamming in our faces, we have new opportunities. We have completed the challenges of youth and middle age. We have raised children, supported a family, and met the demands of a career. Now that, or most of it, is behind us.

Older people have more time and more choices than ever before. Usually the financial pressures are less than in earlier years. We are freer to strike out in new directions, to try new things.

Our responses to challenges in the closing decades of our lives could make the later years the most fulfilling of all.

Seniors have problems, fears and complaints. This book addresses seventy-five of them with hope-filled responses that come from God's Word, the Bible. We lose some things as we grow older, but there are trade-offs. We gain as much as we lose. We may lose some short-term memory, but our reasoning powers improve and we profit from the perspective that comes from decades of experience.

The changes we sense from advancing years are much less important than our attitude toward them. We do not lose the power to choose our responses to life. No one can take from us the right to trust God, to love, and to encourage others.

People in later life achieve remarkable things. In his eighties, Michelangelo was sculpting in the Sistine Chapel. The German poet Goethe completed his greatest drama, "Faust," at age eighty-two. Grandma Moses learned to paint in her seventies.

When he was seventy-three, John Wesley preached fifteen sermons a week. He wrote at that time, "I am far abler to preach than when I was three and twenty."

And when does learning stop? Ask Socrates, who began learning to play a musical instrument when he was eighty. Ask Cato, the Roman consul, who set out to learn Greek at the same age.

Ask the hundreds of thousands of senior citizens who enroll in college courses or undertake educational tours each year.

The advancing years offer us new opportunities to experience God. Our church services may seem predictable, but most of us haven't begun to mine the riches of God's Word, the Bible. We have so much more to learn about the power of prayer. Our senior years are a wonderful time to move to new encounters with God which will continue through eternity.

The Lord promises His children that the last years of our lives would be good ones. "Even to your old age and gray hairs, I am he, I am he who will sustain you" (Isaiah 46:4).

I want to thank my wife, Norma, and five writer friends, Eileen, Freya, Joan, Louise, and Vivian for reading this manuscript and making valuable suggestions.

Willard A. Scofield

PART I

Developing a Positive Spiritual Attitude

1.
"I WISH THE BIBLE COULD PROVIDE THE HELP AND GUIDANCE FOR ME THAT IT SEEMS TO DO FOR SOME PEOPLE."

The Bible can do that for you!

Whether or not you adopt a plan to read the entire Bible, you can acquaint yourself with key verses and chapters that will nourish your soul.

Every believer should be acquainted with these key passages.

The Ten Commandments - *Exodus 20, Deuteronomy 6*
The Beatitudes - *Matthew 5:1-12*
The Lord's Prayer - *Matthew 6:9-13*
The Great Commandments - *Matthew 22:34-40*
The Great Commission - *Matthew 28:16-20*
The Parable of the Prodigal Son - *Luke 15:11-32*
The Parable of the Good Samaritan - *Luke 10:25-37*
The Story of the Death and Resurrection of Jesus -
    Matthew 26-28, Mark 14-16, Luke 22-24, John 18-21
The Love Chapter - *1 Corinthians 13*

Also, it is desirable to know passages that address special needs. When people who are suffering or dying request a Bible reading, most often they choose Psalm 23.

When you are dismayed about how bad people prosper, let David tell you his answer in Psalm 73.

When you feel that you are challenged by spiritual forces with which you cannot cope, Ephesians 6:10-20 is a passage that describes the whole armor of God.

When you are worried, Matthew 6:25-34 has words that you should read and reread.

There are probably at least 300 powerful, individual verses that address specific life situations. They will provide you with comfort and encouragement. Jesus used single verses to meet His spiritual needs. When facing temptations on the mountain, He answers Satan with the words, "It is written..." Paul quotes verses from the Old Testament in his writings. One example is Paul's quotation from Isaiah 64:4 in l Corinthians 2:9, "No eye has seen, no ear has heard, no mind has conceived what God has prepared for those who love him."

Many Christians have found it useful to memorize key verses that address special needs. They sometimes repeat them before retiring at night or when they rise in the morning. We should know several verses that relate to the heart of the Christian faith: man's sin, God's love, the way to receive Christ, and the changed life in Christ. Romans 3:23, John 3:16, Romans l0:9,10 and 2 Corinthians 5:17 point to these truths.

When we sin, we should be aware of 1 John l:9, "If we confess our sins, he is faithful and just and will forgive us our sins and purify us from all unrighteousness."

When we are tempted to fall back on our good works for assurance of salvation, we need Ephesians 2:8,9, "For it is by grace that you have been saved, through faith — and this not from yourselves, it is the gift of God — not by works so that no one can boast."

We also need some verses that will help us tap into God's power. A good one is Philippians 4:19, "And my God will meet all your needs according to his glorious riches in Christ Jesus."

Feel free to use a part of a verse as in Psalm 55:22, "Cast your cares on the Lord and he will sustain you..."

Paul's words in Philippians 4:11 have been a blessing to many. "... I have learned to be content whatever the circumstances."

Many who pass through a time of suffering find refreshment in the words from Psalm 30:5, " ... weeping may remain for a night, but rejoicing comes in the morning."

Select a dozen verses and memorize them. Or, write them in calligraphy and pin them on the wall. Or, paste them on the refrigerator door. Or, put them in your car. Let their messages seep into your soul.

Here are more good verses to check out:

Romans 12:2	Philippians 4:13
Matthew 7:7	Isaiah 55:3
Luke 18:27	John 14:27
Proverbs 3:5	2 Timothy 1:7

When Jesus talked about His teaching, He said, "I have told you this so that my joy may be in you and that your joy may be complete" (John 15:11).

The Bible is an exciting, joy-filled book.

2.
"I AM ASHAMED THAT I HAVEN'T READ THE ENTIRE BIBLE. I'VE TRIED SEVERAL TIMES, BUT I NEVER FINISH."

God still loves you! You are His child even if you haven't read the entire Bible.

But if you are interested in reading the entire Bible, we may reflect on reasons why people don't make it and offer a suggestion as to how to succeed.

Frequently, people follow a plan to read the Bible in a year. Such a program requires a person to read several chapters a day. That may require too much time in one's daily schedule. Various things come up calling for postponement of the readings, and eventually the project is abandoned.

Long stretches of material in the Bible are hard to understand. Some passages may seem to have no relevance to one's personal life.

Another problem is that reading several chapters a day may mean taking on more teaching than one can absorb. Yes, you can say you've done your readings for the day, but that is a hollow victory if those passages have not nourished your soul.

If you want to undertake the reading of the entire Bible, here is a suggestion that may enable you to succeed.

Instead of trying to read several chapters a day, why not try to read thirty-five verses a day, twenty from the Old Testament and fifteen from the New Testament, Psalms, and Proverbs. At that pace, you will complete the Bible in two-and-one-half years. You will be more likely to keep up with your readings and to understand what you read.

The suggested number of verses are averages. If your goal is to average twenty verses a day from the Old Testament, you might read twenty-five to complete a paragraph or story, or the right place to stop might be at the end of fourteen verses.

This plan balances the readings. Although you will find wonderful passages in the Old Testament, these readings will usually be harder to understand. But you will also be reading from the New Testament, Psalms, and Proverbs, which are more likely to have soul-building materials. You could complete one New Testament book, then move on to the Psalms for two weeks. Then continue with another New Testament book, and then back to Psalms for another two weeks. When you have completed the Psalms, alternate your New Testament books with fifteen verses from the book of Proverbs.

Most of the time, you will complete your thirty-five verses in less than ten minutes.

You will improve your chances for understanding the Bible by using a modern translation with notes. The New International Version Study Bible is an excellent Bible. You will find that the brief notes on many verses are just what you need to clear up problems.

Even with a study Bible, you will come to passages that make you say, "Wow, I never knew that was in the Bible." Or, "Why did God tell people to do that?"

Such reactions will lead you to reflect on the differences in the life and culture of people in Bible times and on such ideas as the progressive revelation of God's truth. Even then, you will not completely understand everything you read.

But, you will also have an exciting spiritual experience as you read the entire Bible. You will read stories that are seldom or never mentioned from the pulpit, but which carry great spiritual value. You will encounter people such as Job and Elijah who faced the worst that life could bring and whose victories of faith teach wonderful lessons. You will gain a panoramic view of God's great plan of salvation, its preparation in the Old Testament and its fulfillment in the New Testament.

Approach the Bible prayerfully in the spirit of the Psalmist who said, "Open my eyes that I may see wonderful things in your law" (Psalm 119:18).

As you read, ask, "Is God speaking to me in some way through these words? Is there a promise here for me? Is there a duty for me to fulfill?"

Use a marker to highlight verses you find helpful.

The Bible will change the quality of your life. You will understand the meaning of the verse, "Your word is a lamp to my feet and a light for my path" (Psalm 119:105).

3.

"DO YOU THINK THAT GOD REALLY GUIDES IN DECISION MAKING? IF SO, HOW DOES HE DO THAT?"

We will always be making decisions. Middle aged and older persons have to decide about early retirement, keeping a home or entering a retirement community, living with someone or living alone and many others. We wonder:

> Will my life be better or worse if I do this?
> Can this be right when it seems so hard to do?
> Am I being fair to my family?
> Can God guide me through these questions?

David thought so. He said in Psalm 27:11, "Teach me your way, O Lord; lead me in a straight path."

Here are several guideposts for finding God's will in the hours of decision.

1. The Bible, God's Word, gives clear teaching that helps us make decisions. One such guide is in 2 Corinthians 6:14, "Do not be yoked together with unbelievers." That applies to such situations as marriage, business partnerships, or perhaps even choosing a retirement community. We live in the world and we can make friends with all kinds of people. But in deciding about our most intimate relationships, we should choose believers.

Biblical principles are often general and we must make the specific applications. How do we do that?

2. Many Christians seek signs when making a decision — an unexpected job opportunity, a seeming chance meeting with a stranger that suggests the possibility of a new relationship. Some even put out a "fleece" as Gideon did to challenge God to indicate His will. Gideon put a fleece on the road and asked the Lord to give a positive signal by putting dew on the fleece while the surrounding earth remained dry (Judges 6:36-40). Christians sometimes do the same thing, challenging the Lord to make something happen in a certain way by a certain time. "If I don't get a telephone call from him in two weeks, I'll consider that the Lord has said, 'No.'"

God may respond to our pleas for a sign by opening and closing doors. But God is sovereign, and we cannot force Him to act on our schedule. Our impatience for a sign may lead us astray.

3. God often speaks to us through Christian friends who are not emotionally involved in our decision. They may see elements in a situation that escape us. Many find guidance in support groups where people pray together and listen to each other's needs.

For many years Quakers have had "meetings for clearness" where trusted friends come together to help people think through decisions about things like marriage or a career change. Anyone may assemble a group of believers to listen and give counsel. If there is consensus on a course of action, this may be an indication of God's will.

4. In the final analysis we must make the decision. The signs may be mixed and so may be the advice of our friends. Even if they are clear, we may be convinced that the Lord is leading in a different direction.

The most important elements in our decision making are an understanding of ourselves, our vocation, our knowledge of our gifts, our sense of God's leading, and an inner feeling of peace about a course of action.

We can follow our hearts because we have been instructed in the Scriptures and we have the Holy Spirit. The Spirit can warm our hearts to some project. God's Spirit can guide our reasoning powers as we contemplate a change. We can trust the Holy Spirit to inform our minds and hearts as we ponder and reflect. He will lead us to a decision that will bring us joy.

There is a wonderful promise in Psalm 37:4: "Delight yourself in the Lord and he will give you the desires of your heart."

Augustine said: "Love God and do as you please." When those words are understood correctly, they are gloriously true. As we trust in the Lord, He does give us the desires of our hearts.

4.
"I WONDER WHAT HEAVEN WILL BE LIKE. DOES THE BIBLE TELL US MUCH ABOUT THAT?"

It *is* important to think about heaven. As Phillips Brooks put it, "We may live nobly now, because we shall live forever." The Bible tells us some things about heaven although not all we would like to know.

Jesus said that there would be a special place for each of us in heaven and that we would be with Him (John 14:3). What we understand dimly now will be understood fully because we shall see Jesus face to face (1 Corinthians 13:12).

What do the harps and golden streets mean? Are the writers of Scripture using the most extravagant symbols to point to something beyond our grasp? When the Bible says, "no more night, no more sea, no more tears," it suggests that there is something magnificent that words cannot describe. It might be something like telling a person who had never been outside of Minnesota about a tropical paradise — no more snow, no more ice, no more freezing cold. It will be wonderful — we must wait for the details.

A clue to understanding what is in store for us in heaven is the fact that eternal life begins now. "Whoever believes in the Son *has* eternal life..." (John 3:36a). In Christ, we have a new quality of life which we begin to experience here and which will continue through all eternity.

What are some of the qualities of new life in Christ?

Think of moments when you have felt totally and completely accepted. You could speak freely. You could be yourself. You were surrounded by loving people to whom you could express yourself without fear. Others affirmed you and loved you. You were as happy about the accomplishments of others as you were about your own. That is a glimpse of heaven.

Think of the most productive, the most satisfying work you have ever done. You were fully engaged. You employed your gifts and talents to the utmost. Paid or not, you reveled in that work. That is the nature of our calling in Christ now and forever.

Think of having our life and work judged in absolute fairness. On earth, a few people acquire enormous publicity and rewards. Multitudes who work as hard or harder receive modest recognition. The sadness of job terminations, forced retirements, other people getting credit for what we did — that will be over. The rewards will be honest — exactly what we deserve.

Think of endless possibilities for learning. What we know of the vastness of the universe suggests challenges of continuing exploration and research. One scientist wrote that he felt like a child playing with pebbles and shells on the seashore while the immense ocean of truth extended itself unexplored before him.

Have you experienced the joy of reconciliation? Think of throwing your arms around someone from whom you had been estranged and enjoying fellowship with that person again. In heaven we shall experience love and reconciliation in ways we have never known here.

The New Testament speaks of heaven as a time of singing praises to God. In Revelation 14:3 John says, "And they sang a new song before the throne..." Think of the most stirring choir you have ever heard. Multiply that thrill by a million. Think of a choir of Jews and Arabs, African Americans and Anglo Americans, Japanese and Koreans united to sing praises to the Lord.

Think of the purest, the loveliest, the most satisfying, the most joyous experiences here on earth. They are hints of heaven.

God has prepared beautiful things for those who believe.

5.
"SOME OF MY FRIENDS ARE PASSING AWAY. I WONDER WHETHER I WILL EVER SEE THEM AGAIN."

Most of us have wondered about that. While the Bible doesn't address the question directly, there is evidence that we will see our loved ones again.

Moses and Elijah maintained their personal identity as they appeared before Jesus and the three disciples on the Mount of Transfiguration (Matthew 17:1-13).

In Matthew 22:31,32, Jesus quotes the words of God in Exodus 3:6, "But about the resurrection of the dead — have you not read what God said to you, 'I am the God of Abraham, the God of Isaac, and the God of Jacob'? He is not the God of the dead but of the living." God continues to be the God of Abraham, Isaac, and Jacob hundreds of years after they died. These patriarchs are alive in God's presence and their identities remain.

In the love chapter, 1 Corinthians 13, Paul says: "Now we see but a poor reflection as in a mirror; then we shall see face to face. Now I know in part; then I shall know fully, even as I am fully known" (13:12). Paul believed that after death our personal life would continue and that we would be known as we are known in this life.

The most important evidence is the resurrection of Jesus Christ. His resurrection body was different in some ways, but after their initial shock, Jesus' disciples did recognize Him. He shared a breakfast with them (John 21:10-14) and He invited Thomas to feel his side which had been pierced with a spear (John 20:27). The resurrected Jesus was more than a spirit.

"Look at my hands and my feet. It is I myself! Touch me and see; a ghost does not have flesh and bones, as you see I have" (Luke 24:39). The disciples' experience was so vivid and real that many of them were willing to give their lives for their risen Savior.

That gives us a clue about our spiritual bodies. There will be differences appropriate to a new mode of existence, but there will be a continuity from this life to the next.

If Christ, as Paul says, was to become the first fruits of them that believe (1 Corinthians 15:20), it is reasonable to believe that Christ's resurrection body will be the model for our resurrection experience. Our personal identity will be preserved in a transformed body. Jesus was recognized by others and so will we.

The resurrection will take place at the end of time. Meanwhile we have the assurance that our loved ones have a real existence in which they are known to God and to others. As Paul said, "We are confident, I say, and would prefer to be away from the body and at home with the Lord" (2 Corinthians 5:8).

When we leave this earth, we will leave our loved ones for a little while. At that very time we will be welcomed in heaven by family members and friends and by Jesus Christ.

What a happy reunion that will be!

6.

"I HAVE A FRIEND WHO IS ALWAYS SAYING 'PRAISE THE LORD.' THAT SEEMS A LITTLE EXTREME TO ME."

It may seem awkward to say that all the time, but your friend is on to something important. The key to experiencing God's power is to have an attitude of praise for everything in our lives.

These are things for which some people expressed their thanks:

- walking along a beach in your bare feet
- a bonfire by the lake
- a chocolate milkshake
- singing praise choruses in church
- sending out for pizza on a Friday night
- carrying cups of coffee out to the deck
- sunrises and sunsets
- the soft feel of cotton sheets

Make your own list, and practice praising the Lord. Even though it may not seem appropriate to say praise words in a taxi cab or at the supermarket checkout, you can mentally thank the Lord for a safe driver, for good roads, and a multitude of good foods to choose from.

David was the master of praise in the Bible. He praised God for planning his life before he was born. He praised Him for his future when he would dwell in the house of the Lord forever. He thought about nature and praised God for that — for the sun that knows when to go down, for the moon that marks the seasons, for water and green grass for the cattle. And he thanked God for the forgiveness he had received. "As far as the east is from the west, so far has he removed our transgressions from us" (Psalm 103:12).

But can we praise God for things that seem evil in our lives? Spiritual maturity is coming to the place where we can say, "Lord, you know how terrible I feel about this. But I know that you can take this mess and make something good from it. I praise you for where I am right now because I know that you are in charge."

That attitude is based on our acceptance that God is present and powerful. Because God is in control, we can move ahead with confidence.

In praising God for the present, we open ourselves to His power.

A man named Matthew Henry did just that when he was robbed. He said:

"I am thankful that it never happened before.

I am thankful that they took my money and not my life. Though they took it all, it wasn't much.

And I am thankful that it was I who was robbed and that I was not the one who robbed."

He turned what seemed like a calamity into a blessing. We can do that too.

7.
"SOMETIMES I WAKE UP IN THE MIDDLE OF THE NIGHT AND WONDER IF I'M REALLY A CHILD OF GOD."

At one time or another many Christians lack assurance of their salvation. Why should this be?

1. One reason may be the rarity of a gift that is totally free. It's so different from the way we think. When someone receives an honor, a raise in salary, or a promotion, we talk about whether she deserved it or not. But the free invitation to enter God's Kingdom is available to everyone — the rich man, the poor man, the beggar man and the thief. Strange, but true.

13

To gain assurance of our salvation, we need to return to the Word of God and let its message sink into our souls. The Gospel is the story of God acting on our behalf. "But God demonstrates his own love for us in this: While we were still sinners, Christ died for us" (Romans 5:8). Another pointed reference to God's grace is: "For it is by grace you have been saved, through faith — and this not from yourselves, it is the gift of God — not by works, so that no one can boast" (Ephesians 2:8,9).

2. The guilt trips people lay on us tend to break down our assurance.

We've heard a preacher or some church member say: "A real Christian does this or that..." We haven't been doing it and the question comes to our minds, "Am I really a Christian?"

When they are angry, some of our friends or family members repeat mean words such as, "Fine Christian you are!" We suspect that they may be right.

Some people with a strict upbringing still have some form of the command, "Measure up," resounding in their subconscious minds and those words do battle with the Good News: "By grace you have been saved."

The therapy is the same — the Word of God. "Whoever believes in the Son has eternal life..." (John 3:36a).

3. Still another problem is that we feel badly about our spiritual defeats. We can't get control of our tempers, we have habits that we've never conquered, we feel guilty about failed relationships. Shouldn't Christians be sweeter, nicer people? What's wrong?

Two things are worth noting here.

The fact that we are troubled about the quality of our Christian lives shows that we are spiritually alive and care about what God wants for us. People who are not Christians are not concerned about that.

Also, we have the promise of God: "If we confess our

sins, he is faithful and just and will forgive us our sins and purify us from all unrighteousness" (1 John 1:9).

The key to assurance is returning to the Word of God. We are God's children because we have received the gift of salvation by faith. When in doubt, repeat these words: "That if you confess with your mouth, 'Jesus is Lord,' and believe in your heart that God raised him from the dead, you will be saved" (Romans 10:9).

God said it! I believe it! That settles it!

And it may help to repeat the words of a hymn, sung by many as they entered the Kingdom of God.

> "Amazing grace, how sweet the sound
> That saved a wretch like me.
> I once was lost, but now am found,
> Was blind, but now I see."

As he neared death, the author of that hymn, John Newton, said: "My memory is nearly gone, but I remember two things, that I am a great sinner and that Christ is a great Savior."

8.
"I'VE NEVER UNDERSTOOD WHAT PAUL MEANT WHEN HE SAID, 'PRAY WITHOUT CEASING.'"

These words from the King James Version of 1 Thessalonians 5:17 might be taken to mean that a person should be on his knees in prayer at all times — an obvious impossibility.

A better rendering is found in the NIV version which says simply, "pray continually."

That suggests several ways of thinking about prayer:

We should never give up on prayer.

We should be constantly in an attitude of prayer, open to God's leading.

We can pray in all sorts of places, at any time, for all kinds of people. We can pray in two-minute, one-minute, even ten-second segments.

Frank Laubach, a pioneer in developing literacy programs, talked about flashing prayers at people. He often did this on a subway or bus. He looked at the other person and asked God to work in his life. He said that sometimes the person looked up and smiled.

Let us think of situations which offer opportunities for short prayers:

We can make a two-second prayer as we pick up the telephone to call a person or before we step into his office. "Lord, make this conversation useful. Help me to remember the things I planned to say."

Waiting for a traffic light to change usually involves less than thirty seconds, although it seems a lot longer. That's enough time to think of a friend who is hurting, and to make a short prayer, asking God to touch her life.

Who are those people in the dentist's office staring across the room at you? Do they have problems? Is one of them facing a test today? Ask God to work in their lives.

Some of us wake up early in the morning, maybe an hour before the alarm goes off. This is a time to repeat the names of people on our prayer list.

"Work in Jon's life, Lord."

"Lord, help Joan, You know what she needs."

Many of us walk or jog. This could be a time for prayer, perhaps for confession of sin. Just as the exercise is cleansing our body, our confession cleanses our souls.

As the medieval monk, Brother Lawrence, practiced the presence of God amid the pots and pans of his kitchen, we can aim short prayers at our fellow workers as we tap away on our computers.

When I told a young typist that we were getting some good inquiries from the letters she was preparing, she said,

"I'm not surprised. As I've typed each letter, I've said a prayer for the person receiving it."

It is especially important that Christians pray for their pastors. These servants of the Lord need our prayers for deliverance from temptation and for God's power as they preach and teach in our churches.

After a young preacher had settled into his church in Philadelphia, he was visited one evening by a member of his church. This layman gave the preacher this candid statement, "You are not a strong preacher, but a little group of us have agreed to gather every Sunday morning to pray for you." That small group grew to nearly a thousand people. The pastor was J. Wilbur Chapman, who became one of the most effective preachers of his generation.

Those faithful people were giving their pastor the greatest gift. When we think, "All we can do is pray," follow it up with these words: "This is the most important thing we can do."

9.
"HOW CAN I BE MORE EFFECTIVE IN PRAYING FOR OTHERS?"

Jesus taught us that God wants to hear our prayers. We do not have to learn special prayer formulas to get His attention. Nor do we have to be super Christians. Here are some thoughts to guide us in praying for others.

In choosing who to pray for, we think first of people in our circle who have special needs. If a friend asks us to pray for her, that is a challenge we should not ignore. Many Christians feel that the Lord gives them a burden or a special prayer concern for a certain person. If your mind is pulled to the need of a man or woman, if someone's problem concerns you deeply, that is a person for whom you should intercede.

As you pray for others, begin by focusing on God. Praise God for His love for the person who is the object of your prayers. Thank the Lord that He is already at work in your friend's life.

Then talk to God about your friend's need. That may be more involved than you understand. So you will ask the Lord to do what is right. A woman may need a new job, but there may be changes that should take place in her life before she is ready for a new job. A good prayer might be, "Lord, you know that Lois needs a job and a lot of other things as well. Please work in her life."

If you don't know what your friend needs, just mention her name and ask the Lord to work in her life. It is well to thank the Lord in advance for His answer.

Ask others to pray for Lois. Jesus taught that there is special power when more than one person prays for a specific need (Matthew 18:19,20).

Let your friend know that you are praying for her. Sometimes the Lord may use you to answer your own prayers. Think of practical ways you may help her.

Most prayers are not answered instantly. God works in His time and in His way. When there seems to be no answer, let us remember that outward appearances are sometimes the opposite of what is really taking place in a person's life.

When we don't know how to pray for a person, or when we don't see the results we had hoped for, many people make what is called a "prayer of relinquishment." It might be something like this: "Dear Lord, we have prayed for Dan so many times. The doctors seem to have tried everything. At this time, we commit him to You. We accept whatever Your will is for his life. We know that You love him and that You will do what is right. In Jesus' name we pray. Amen."

When answers come, let us praise the Lord for His responses to our prayers. These answers will encourage us as we continue to intercede for others.

God wants us to pray. He listens and He will respond. He loves us because we are His children.

10.
"ARE THERE CONDITIONS TO RECEIVING ANSWERS TO OUR PRAYERS?"

Yes, there are.

The most prominent one is Jesus' teaching that an unforgiving spirit interferes with our relationship with God. In the Lord's prayer, Jesus says, "Forgive us our debts, as we also have forgiven our debtors" (Matthew 6:12). Then, at the end of the prayer, to emphasize the importance of this point, He adds, "For if you forgive men when they sin against you, your heavenly Father will also forgive you. But if you do not forgive men their sins, your Father will not forgive your sins" (Matthew 6:14,15).

Also in the Sermon on the Mount, Jesus says, "Therefore, if you are offering your gift at the altar and there remember that your brother has something against you, leave your gift there in front of the altar. First go and be reconciled to your brother; then come and offer your gift" (Matthew 5:23,24).

We can be religious, attend church, tithe, do 101 good things, but if we are holding something in our hearts against another person, we are cutting off God's power.

It's something like the kink in my garden hose. No matter how high the pressure, the water won't go through until I get the kink out of the hose.

Regardless of the nature of the wrong, we need to let the person we resent know that we want to restore the relationship. We are not saying that she is right. She may not accept our overture. The important thing is that we have done what Jesus commanded. Regardless of her reaction, we can pray for her health and prosperity.

Do other sins block our prayers to God? They can. "But your iniquities have separated you from your God; your sins have hidden his face from you, so that he will not hear" (Isaiah 59:2).

Should we pray if we have bad habits, addictions, a problem with our tempers? Of course we should, but God should also hear our confession and our prayer for victory over these habits.

We certainly don't have to be perfect to receive answers to our prayers. If that were so, no prayer would be answered.

A final point is important. It is inappropriate to pray for something that would transgress God's law. Any prayer whose fulfillment would do harm to another person would be wrong.

Many prayers end with the words, "Through Jesus Christ our Lord." Those are not magic words to insure the safe arrival of our prayer at God's throne. It's a way of saying, "I've thought about what Christ wants in my life. I know His standards, and I want the answer to this prayer to be pleasing to Him."

In committing our prayers to God in this way, we are also saying, "I am willing to accept 'no' as an answer so that I can hear your higher 'yes' in the future."

That clears the channel.

Then we are ready for answered prayers.

11.

"JESUS MAKES SOME AMAZING PROMISES ABOUT PRAYER. THEY ALMOST SEEM TOO GOOD TO BE TRUE."

Indeed they do! One of them is found in Mark 11:24. "Therefore I tell you, whatever you ask for in prayer, believe that you have received it, and it will be yours."

Another way the Bible puts this is, "...You do not have, because you do not ask God" (James 4:2).

A stunning truth! When we pray, we can count on receiving answers. We change, the people in our world may change, some of our circumstances may change.

A family whose mission work my wife and I had decided to support wrote to us after receiving our check. "The day your check arrived, we were praying for a new supporter."

Coincidence? Maybe. But that reminded me of the words of a former Archbishop of Canterbury, "When I pray, coincidences occur, when I fail to pray, they don't."

To experience answers to prayer, begin with simple requests about things you believe God wants to happen in your life. Write them down in a notebook and include the day you made the request. Leave space for the date the answer comes.

My wife and I did this in a small group. People made prayer requests about

- problems at work,
- earaches,
- children passing exams,
- getting more Tupperware parties,
- the grace to forgive a mother.

It was exciting to record the answers.

To claim God's power in prayer, let us think about Jesus' practice of thanking God for the answer before it happens.

Before He fed the five thousand, Jesus gave thanks (John 6:11).

When He was about to raise Lazarus from the dead, He said, "Father, I thank you that you have heard me" (John 11:41).

In praying, use your imagination in claiming God's promises. Picture in your mind His mighty work.

In talking about confession and forgiveness, one pastor challenged his congregation, "Now picture yourself carrying your burdens of guilt to the foot of the cross. Place them there, one by one, and look up at Jesus, acknowledging your need for forgiveness. Then accept it — and walk away leaving your burdens behind."

Let us use our imaginations as we intercede for others. Let us picture Jesus standing beside the bed of a loved one in the operating room. Let us imagine Jesus accompanying our son as he goes for an interview for a scholarship. Let us see in our minds the Lord bringing about a reconciliation between two estranged persons.

Ask and you will receive — it seems almost too good to be true. But that's what Jesus promised. He wants to hear and answer our prayers.

12.
"BUT SOME PRAYERS ARE NOT ANSWERED. WHY?"

That is a troubling question that has been asked in many ways.

On the back of one prayer card, a man wrote, "Where was God when the Nazis were gassing six million Jews?"

We have prayed for the healing of friends with cancer. Many of them have died. Why weren't our prayers answered?

Much has been spoken and written about this, but nothing seems to completely answer our questions.

Perhaps some guidance will come in thinking about Jesus' prayers. Is it shocking to suggest that some of His prayers were not answered?

Did Jesus pray for His disciples? Did He pray for Judas? Were His prayers for Judas answered?

We assume that Jesus prayed about every ministry He

undertook. Yet, we read in Matthew 13:58 about Jesus' ministry in His hometown. "And he did not do many miracles there because of their lack of faith."

In a way, it seems strange that some of Jesus' prayers did not have a response. However, why shouldn't that have been so? Jesus passed through every experience that we pass through. We suffer through the ambiguities of seemingly unanswered prayers. Why shouldn't our great high priest have suffered through them too?

These passages do, however, give us clues about unanswered prayers. They suggest that answers to prayers made on behalf of others relate to their openness and receptivity to God's work. It seems that God does not override the wills of rebellious people. That doesn't mean He has stopped working, but that His response will come later in a way we may not have expected.

In the Garden of Gethsemane, Jesus said, "My Father, if it is possible, may this cup be taken from me. Yet not as I will, but as you will" (Matthew 26:39). Jesus prayed for deliverance from death, yet He left the matter in God's hands. Jesus died on Calvary's cross, and we know that God used Christ's death to complete His great plan of salvation.

That may be the key to understanding unanswered prayers. God is at work, and some day we will see that His answer is a beautiful part of a design we have not yet grasped.

The story of a man named Scott Lawrence is an encouragement to those who grapple with unanswered prayer. Scott Lawrence, who lived at the beginning of this century, had a career on Broadway. He was a song writer and musician. He had recognition, money — everything except the woman he wanted, Victoria Barnes.

Scott pleaded with Victoria to marry him. She loved him, but Scott wasn't a Christian and he didn't want a Christian lifestyle. As he proposed, he offered her the fiction that many women have been unable to resist, "Vicky, you can change me."

Vicky replied, "Scott, only God can change you." They separated. She played his songs on the piano and she prayed. She sent his name to others for prayer.

Scott went his own way. He became addicted to alcohol and cocaine. Later he began stealing to support his addictions. He spent six months in jail.

Sometimes he thought of Vicky's words, "We can have a beautiful life together, Scotty. But you've got to turn to God. He loves you and so do I."

One night Scott Lawrence stumbled into the Pacific Garden Mission in Chicago. The superintendent's wife talked with him about Christ. Together they read from the Bible, "But as many as received him, to them gave he power to become the sons of God, even to them that believe on his name" (John 1:12 KJV).

That night Scott Lawrence received Christ as his Savior. After some times of painful readjustment, he began writing gospel songs, some of which are sung to this day.

This story has a lovely ending. Scott and Victoria met again and married. They had several wonderful years together before Scott died.

After his death, Victoria wrote to the people at Pacific Garden Mission. "When you feel discouraged, remember Scott and gain new courage. Say over and over again, 'With Christ's help, it can be done, it has been done, and it will be done again.'"

Stories like that encourage us. We may not see such happy endings to some of our prayers, but Scott Lawrence's life does remind us that God is at work. Some day, in this life or in another, we will see His answers and thank Him.

13.
"I HEAR ABOUT PEOPLE PRAYING ALL NIGHT. WHAT DO THEY SAY? I CAN PRAY FOR EVERY-THING I WANT IN TEN MINUTES."

This question brings us to the heart of the prayer experience, whether we pray for a few minutes or several hours.

Prayer is much more than just passing on several requests. It is as Isaiah said, "waiting upon the Lord" (Isaiah 40:31 KJV). But what does that mean?

1. Prayer is an opportunity to relax in the presence of God and imagine Jesus working in your life.

Think of Jesus saying to you, "My peace I give to you." Imagine Him smiling at you.

Think of your tensions, resentments and fears as dirt on your body that need to be washed away. Imagine an angel pouring a pitcher of warm water over your body. Now you feel clean.

Picture Jesus walking along the road with you. When you come to an intersection, Jesus points to the right and says, "This is the way we should go."

2. Spend time talking, not about your requests, but just telling the Lord how much you love Him. Thank Him for sending Jesus to die for you. Say things like:

"Father, Your power is with me everywhere I go."

"Lord, You are wonderful."

"Jesus, there's nothing in my life that is too big for You to handle."

"Thank you, Lord, for the answers you will give to my prayers this night."

3. Then talk to the Lord about the things that concern you. Pray simply — no pious language, no "thees" and "thous."

"Lord, You know I can't stand Audrey, change me."

"We've prayed so often that Bob will find a job. Keep his spirits up."

"Help Sharon cope with those kids in her preschool class."

When you don't know how to pray for a person, just say something like,

"You know Debbie, Lord, please help her."

4. In your prayer time, plan for periods of silence. Let your mind become like a blank slate. You might begin this period by saying, "Lord, take away my desires, my preconceived notions, I just want to listen to you." As you listen, God may give you an insight, an idea, you've never had before. A verse may come to mind that speaks to your need. You are waiting on the Lord.

If nothing comes, just continue to wait.

5. Intersperse these moments of silence with affirmations from the Bible.

"The Lord is my shepherd, I shall not be in want" (Psalm 23:1).

"He who dwells in the shelter of the Most High will rest in the shadow of the Almighty" (Psalm 91:1).

"Cast all your anxiety on him because he cares for you" (1 Peter 5:7).

Then be silent again, let the Lord speak.

6. As you come to dilemmas, situations that seem impossible, make prayers of relinquishment. One such prayer might be,

> " Lord, I can't.
> You can.
> Please do.
> Thank you."

Jesus prayed all night and He didn't just repeat the same words over and over again. He condemned that practice. He waited upon the Lord and came from His prayers ready to perform the mightiest works the world has ever known.

Prayer is more than talking, it is coming into the presence of God. It is leaving refreshed, clean, confident that your life is safe in the hands of the One who loves you.

14.
"I'VE HEARD PEOPLE TELL ABOUT HOW GOD SPOKE TO THEM AT A SPIRITUAL RETREAT. I'D LIKE TO HAVE THAT KIND OF EXPERIENCE."

You might return from a time apart with God with a whole new view of your life.

After feeding the multitudes with five loaves and two fishes, Jesus sent the people away and went up to the mountain to pray (Matthew 14:23).

Jesus delivered the teaching of the Sermon on the Mount to His disciples in a setting that we might call a retreat.

Opportunities for retreats abound. Your denomination may have a conference center with retreats for college youth, singles, young families, men, women, and senior citizens.

Among the numerous non-denominational centers is one in California which has sponsored retreats for such specialized groups as firefighters and their families. On the other side of the country, a center in Pennsylvania has arranged retreats for the newly unemployed.

In most large cities, there are marriage encounter weekends to help couples of all ages enrich their marriages.

If you want to consider attending a retreat, these are some things to think about:

1. Whether you spend a weekend or a week at a retreat, it's desirable that you spend the nights away from home. You want to get away from the routine of your daily life, including the TV, newspapers and phone calls. Jesus did His teaching by the lakeside or on a mountain, places where people could see stars and sparrows.

2. Think about whether you would like to go with people you know or to join a large group, many of whom you do not know.

3. What is the retreat's program? Who will be the speakers? What is the theme?

4. Will there be times for prayer and sharing concerns in small groups? These can be the most valuable experiences you can have, and for these times it is often an advantage to be with people you have not previously known.

5. Are there times and places for meditation and reflection? It is in these moments that God may take something from the messages you have heard and help you apply it. Or, you may have an opportunity to reflect upon your life, to hear God telling you what is important and what is not.

It would be possible to arrange a retreat just for yourself or for you and your spouse. A cabin in the wilderness, some tapes of Christian messages and music, a Bible and nothing to do for a day or two but to listen, pray and reflect. Two days like that could turn a light on the dark parts of your life.

Whatever kind of retreat you plan, you may come away saying things like:

"I need a job change — not a new job, but a new way of looking at the one I have now. I have so many new ideas about my work, I can hardly wait to get back."

"Things haven't been right with Diane. I'm going to talk to her when I get home."

"I've never gotten to know those new people coming to church. We're going to invite them to dinner."

"I feel clean after having a chance to confess that sin."

"I have new ideas to fire up our marriage."

"I've been neglecting my aunt in North Dakota. I'll call her."

"I've been too critical of our pastor. It's time for me to begin saying and doing things to encourage him."

If one of these things happened, that could be a turning point in your life.

15.
"WHEN I WAS A YOUNGSTER I THOUGHT ABOUT GOING OVERSEAS AS A MISSIONARY. SOMETIMES I WONDER WHAT A LIFE LIKE THAT WOULD HAVE BEEN LIKE."

You may still be able to find out.

Scores of overseas mission organizations are recruiting volunteers, and most of them are flexible on the matter of age. In recent years, volunteers in their fifties, sixties, and older have performed valuable service in Africa, Asia and Latin America.

Harry and Claudette Martin, who are in their fifties, live in Moscow, Iowa. Harry is a long distance truck driver. Claudette had her own truck dispatching business. They first saw Congo (formerly Zaire) when they visited an uncle and aunt who were career missionaries serving with the Board of International Ministries of American Baptist Churches.

A year after their visit, Harry and Claudette heard that replacements were needed for the mission engineer and his wife while on furlough. Claudette was afraid that God wanted them to become those replacements. These thoughts went through her mind.

"Lord, you know that I don't like that African food."

"Why us? How can I leave my grandkids and water bed?"

"What about my sewing machine and my flowers? And my work?"

"We don't even know French."

"I don't want another attack of malaria."

But Claudette said, "God kept telling me in all kinds of

ways: 'I'll take care of you.'"

And God did take care of them. Harry and Claudette performed valuable service. Harry helped keep the vehicles of the Western Congo Baptist Community running, and Claudette did bookkeeping for the mission.

When they returned to the United States, they became great interpreters of mission work.

Volunteers usually serve in support roles for established mission organizations. They perform such work as teaching English, mechanical repairs, construction, guest house managers, and accounting. Terms of service vary from a few months to two years. Some people serve just a few weeks to give enrichment courses to teachers or to put a new roof on a church.

Volunteers are usually responsible for their transportation, insurance, room and board and other expenses. In some cases, housing and a small stipend are provided.

Many volunteers feel that their time overseas was the greatest experience of their lives. They learned first hand how God is leading His church to take the Gospel to all nations. When they return home, they often make the best interpreters of missions.

The mission agency of your church denomination is the place to start inquiring about the possibilities of overseas service. If your church has no volunteer program, dozens of independent mission societies do.

Some older people have found fulfilling service in the Peace Corps, which works in many countries on projects such as agriculture, fish culture, public health and many others. Some Peace Corps volunteers are assigned to mission stations.

The Bible has no retirement program, no age when our talents and gifts are nullified. At 60, Paul was looking forward to taking the Gospel to Spain.

God may have the greatest years of your life ahead!

16.
"WHEN I HEAR CHRISTIANS TALK ABOUT WINNING SOULS FOR CHRIST, I FEEL GUILTY. I DON'T KNOW THAT I HAVE EVER WON SOMEONE TO CHRIST. "

You may have done more than you think to bring people to the Lord.

Do you have children who are living a Christian life? Regardless of where they made their decisions to enter the Kingdom of God, their Christian parents had the most important influence on their lives.

If you have supported the mission enterprises of your denomination or church, then you share in the rewards of those efforts, many of which are bringing thousands to Christ.

You can think the same way about the work of your local church. If your church has an evangelistic outreach, then you have a part in winning people to Christ. Your money, your support in teaching or administration, your work in preparing supper for a team of visitors all contribute to bringing people to the Lord.

If you have given a word of witness, you may well have had a part in the ultimate conversion of a friend or family member, even though you may never know about it. Jesus made this clear in his reflections to his disciples after meeting with the woman of Samaria. "Thus the saying 'One sows and another reaps' is true. I sent you to reap what you have not worked for. Others have done the hard work, and you have reaped the benefits of their labor" (John 4:37,38).

Another relevant truth is that God gives some people the gift of evangelism. They experience results because God has enabled them to do so. Those who do not have this gift, the rest of us, are called to be witnesses. That means giving

31

expression to our faith when an opportunity comes.

That may mean listening to someone tell you about a problem and saying, "I'm glad you shared that with me, I'm going to pray for a solution."

On other occasions you may share an experience to show how God worked in your life. In listening and sharing like this, you are witnessing without preaching.

Occasionally, people may bring up spiritual questions that you don't feel you can answer. When that happens, you can refer them to someone else, perhaps your pastor.

Or, you could offer the person something to read such as Billy Graham's book *Peace With God*. For people with intellectual objections to the Christian faith, you might suggest books such as *More Than a Carpenter*, by Josh McDowell, or *Mere Christianity*, by C.S. Lewis.

If someone says to you, "Tell me how I can have the faith you have," or "Tell me how I may become a Christian," you may share several key verses that an inquirer should know, and then ask for a decision.

Four key Bible verses unfold simply the way of salvation.

1. John 3:16 sums up God's plan. "For God so loved the world that he gave his one and only Son, that whoever believes in him shall not perish but have eternal life."

2. Romans 3:23 indicates our estrangement from God, "... for all have sinned and fall short of the glory of God...."

3. When Christ died on the Cross, He paid the penalty for our sins. 1 Peter 2:24 tells us, "He himself bore our sins in his body on the tree, so that we might die to sins and live for righteousness; by his wounds you have been healed."

4. Salvation is a gift which is ours for the asking, "Yet to all who received him, to those who believed in his name, he gave the right to become children of God . . ." (John 1:12).

If your friend indicates that she wants to receive Christ as Savior, it would be appropriate to ask her to repeat this prayer after you or to say "Amen" when you have finished saying the prayer. "Father in heaven, I thank You for sending Jesus to die for me. Please forgive my sins. I ask You now to come into my heart so that I may live a life that will please You. In Jesus' name I pray. Amen."

Your friend may want to talk more about the steps to make a decision for Christ. She may raise questions, some of which you don't feel qualified to answer. In that case, a more experienced Christian may be able to help.

Don't be discouraged if the person isn't ready to make a decision. You have sown the seed, and at some time in the future, you or another person may rejoice in seeing your friend become a Christian. Pray for her and keep in touch.

God will honor you for your faithful witness.

17.
"I HAVE TWO CHILDREN WHO SEEM TO CARE NOTHING FOR GOD AND THE CHURCH. THEY WERE RAISED IN THE CHURCH — I WONDER WHAT I DID WRONG."

You are among many parents who ask this question. All of us made mistakes in raising our children. For that, we can receive God's forgiveness and we should forgive ourselves.

But, if we took our children to church and Sunday school, if we exemplified Christian values in the home, if our children heard us pray, then we can rejoice that they did receive Christian training.

We did our part in fulfilling Proverbs 22:6, "Train a child in the way he should go, and when he is old he will not turn from it."

For those who ask, "Why didn't the promised fulfillment occur with my children?" let us consider these points:

1. Our adult children seek to establish an identity separate from ours. Many try to believe and act differently from their parents. Some of those beliefs and actions relate to religion. Once their new identity is secure, our children are free to make their own decisions about spiritual things. Sooner or later, many return to the faith of their parents.

2. We should realize that loyalty to the institutional church is not the same thing as Christian faith. Even if they don't go to church, some of our children pray, and some of them do indeed trust Christ as Savior.

3. Our children cannot get away from the Christian training they received from us. Whatever religious profession they make or do not make, the training they received continues to influence their decisions today.

4. Even when our children seem to have completely rejected their Christian training, they do know the Gospel. They know that they can return to the Lord and some of them will do that, even if it is not in our lifetime.

Is there anything left for us to do? The answer is a resounding yes!

The day has passed when we can bundle our children into a car to go to church and Sunday school. But we can pray for them, and prayer is powerful.

One of the great fathers of the Christian Church was St. Augustine. His writings still influence theologians.

Augustine had a godly mother named Monica who gave him a good Christian training. But, as a young man, he rebelled and lived an immoral life. During these years of rebellion, Augustine's mother continued to pray. She became so well known for her prayers that one bishop told her, "It is not possible that the son of such tears should be lost."

For years Monica's prayers were not answered. On one occasion she prayed that Augustine would not leave for Italy where she feared he would move even farther from the faith.

It seemed that her prayer was not answered — Augustine went to Italy. But it was there that he heard a voice in a garden say: "Take up and read." He took the Bible and read words from Romans 13:13-14 (KJV): "...Not in rioting and drunkenness, not in chambering and wantonness, not in strife and envying. But put ye on the Lord Jesus Christ, and make not provision for the flesh, to fulfill the lusts thereof."

Of this moment, Augustine wrote: "No further would I read, nor needed I, for instantly at the end of this sentence, a light of serenity infused my heart, all the darkness of doubt vanished away."

Although Monica had to wait a long time, the great goal of her prayers, Augustine's salvation, was gloriously realized.

Your prayers for your children are potent — keep praying!

18.
"I GAVE YEARS OF SERVICE TO MY CHURCH. NOW THEY'VE FORGOTTEN ME — NO ONE EVER CALLS."

A church shouldn't forget those who have served faithfully over the years. You are still part of the fellowship of your local church and you should be remembered.

It would be appropriate to call your pastor or a member of the church staff and tell him/her that you would like someone to call. The pastor or a lay person will probably come to encourage you and bring you up to date on the events of the church.

If you have a spiritual problem to discuss, or if you would like to have communion served to you in your home, you have the right to ask the pastor or someone on the pastoral staff to visit you .

If your church doesn't have a systematic way of keeping in touch with shut-ins, you might suggest that the official board think that through. Perhaps your comment will prompt the leaders to develop a plan to keep in touch with the whole body of Christ.

While you have a right to expect the church to keep in touch with you, you can thank the Lord for the opportunities you've had to serve the Church. You will find satisfaction in remembering that the church's outreach today is related to what went on years before. You had an important part in their ministry.

Most important, you were doing that work for the Lord and He will honor your service.

Then, you might think of some ways in which you can continue to participate in your church's ministry.

Shut-ins can have a prayer ministry. Why not take the church directory and pray for two families each day? Although it is not necessary to do so, some people send a card telling the family that they prayed and thought of them.

If you are able, why not ask the church if there is any way you might help at home performing tasks such as collating a newsletter, or addressing and stuffing envelopes?

Does your church record their services? Why not request that they send you a tape of some of the services? Listening will help you feel a part of the church. If the pastor preaches a helpful message, write a note to let him know that. If you appreciated something the choir sang, let the director know that you were inspired. You can be sure she will let choir members know. They will be encouraged.

Although absent from his friends, Paul said to them, "... I have you in my heart..." (Philippians 1:7).

That is what your church should be saying to you.

That is what you want to say to your friends at church.

19.
"I DON'T FEEL LIKE GOING TO CHURCH MUCH ANYMORE, I'VE HEARD IT ALL BEFORE."

Christians who make that comment probably have good reasons for feeling that way. Church services often seem dull, and many sermons are so predictable that they invite people to catch up on their sleep.

But, should we always expect novelty in a worship service?

The purpose of worship is to glorify and honor God. To do that, it is necessary to repeat some eternal truths. That is the reason for the Lord's Supper. 1 Corinthians 11:26 states: "For whenever you eat this bread and drink this cup, you proclaim the Lord's death until he comes."

Baptism, which is observed publicly in most Christian churches, repeats the universal truth that in Christ we receive new life and enter a new community.

The Bible provides an almost inexhaustible supply of truths for the pastor's sermons. But he also has the duty to repeat the heart of the Gospel and some basic themes about Christian discipleship.

To anyone weary of church-going, let us say that it is possible to make every service a grace-filled, creative event.

Think about what is different. A good resolution to make for the church service this Sunday would be: "I am going to learn something I didn't know before, and I am going to meet someone new."

Is there anything new to be found in a familiar Scripture reading?

Recently, I read 1 Timothy 6:11, "... pursue righteousness, godliness, faith, love, endurance and gentleness." Instead of focusing on the virtues, faith, love, etc, I thought about the verb "pursue." Achieving these virtues is a process that may take years.

In listening to the pastor's message, seek one thing that may change your life or thinking for the coming week. Write it on the bulletin. If there is something in his message that is not clear, ask the pastor about it. He will probably be pleased that you were listening closely enough to see the problem. If he seems to omit subjects that you think important, ask him to consider a message on one of these themes.

If you would like to hear the choir repeat a number, tell the leader and some of the members. Because you asked, they may well repeat it.

If public requests for prayer are invited, mention one or two of your needs.

Determine that you will engage one or two people in a brief conversation after the service. If there are new people in church, give them a warm greeting. Tell them something about the church's program.

You should never forget that your presence is an encouragement to others. The writer of Hebrews says, "Let us not give up meeting together, as some are in the habit of doing, but let us encourage one another..." (Hebrews 10:25).

Your attendance at a worship service will encourage others in your congregation. It is something you will never do by listening to a service on TV. In a majority of churches in the United States, the attendance at a worship service is fewer than 100. Your presence will be noted.

If you maintain eye contact with the pastor when he is preaching, he will appreciate that. If you look expectantly at the musicians, you will encourage them. If you are happily participating in the service, other worshippers will catch your enthusiasm.

You can make a difference in your church next Sunday!

20.
"I CAN'T STAND THE NEW MUSIC IN OUR SUNDAY WORSHIP SERVICE. SOMETIMES I FEEL LIKE GETTING UP AND WALKING OUT."

In recent years music has become a divisive issue in many churches.

In some places hymn books have been almost abandoned and people read the words of songs from a screen in front of the church.

Many of the songs projected on the screen are recently composed praise choruses which take a theme and repeat it many times.

In some churches, the traditional choir, which included people of all ages, has been eliminated or limited to occasional service.

Special music comes from instrumental ensembles which seem heavy with brass and drums. Young soloists sing into a microphone with a background of recorded music. They often sing numbers we've never heard before. Some of the music doesn't seem right for the church.

Seniors say, "We miss the old hymns which taught us as much about the faith as the sermons and lessons in Sunday school."

In extreme cases some older people protest by sitting down while the congregation sings the new songs.

How should we think about all of this?

Larger churches sometimes have two services, one traditional and one contemporary. But the majority of churches aren't large enough to divide the congregation into two parts. Also, many people feel there is a loss of community when a congregation has two morning services.

Some seniors think about going to another church where there is a more traditional service. But some of these people have invested years of their lives in their church and they realize they wouldn't be happy some place else.

Many older people just accept the new music saying something like, "If this is what it takes to keep young people in the church, we can put up with it."

That may be a statement that most of us would make.

Perhaps we can go beyond that. We should make an effort to understand the new music that young people want to sing. Most of it does honor God and proclaims, in some way, the Gospel of Christ. We may want to remember that some of the older tunes we love were disdained by traditionalists in other times.

Most churches have a music committee or an official board that supervises the music of the church. Couldn't we suggest that they reflect on the quality of the music? Let them think about the best and the mediocre in contemporary Christian music. As in every art, some forms of contemporary Christian music are superior to others.

Let the music committee think about new ways of using the music we love. Could we look for new arrangements of some of the older hymns? Another problem to be addressed is that many older people in the church have musical gifts. They like to sing in a choir or choral group. Some have done solo work. There are people who play an instrument well. They feel that the Lord isn't finished with them yet. A music committee should think about how their talents might be used.

What about several "old fashioned hymn sing nights" each year? People could select favorite hymns. Older people could present special solo or instrumental selections.

The music committee might think of ways to use seniors' musical gifts in outreach ministries in the community. These might include services at nursing homes, hospitals, missions or prisons.

We know that we have moved into a new era of church

life. We can live with that.

But we still want to sing the music we love. Let the church help us find a way.

21.
"I'VE ALWAYS TRIED TO GIVE A TITHE OF MY INCOME TO THE LORD. I CAN'T DO THAT ANY MORE AND I FEEL BADLY ABOUT IT."

The short answer is that you shouldn't feel badly. God wants you to experience the joy of giving, but He knows your limitations. He honors you for giving what you can.

A statement like this calls for a brief investigation of the Bible's teaching on giving.

Tithing was the standard for giving in the Old Testament, and a blessing was promised to those who followed that standard. (See Malachi 3:10). Jesus mentioned tithing only indirectly when he rebuked people who tithed on everything but neglected the "more important matters of the law" (Matthew 23:23).

The central New Testament teaching on giving is that we are called to offer all of our lives and resources to God. After Paul had outlined the plan of salvation in the first 11 chapters of Romans, he called on his readers to "offer your bodies as living sacrifices, holy and pleasing to God" (Romans 12:1). No longer is it ten percent for God and ninety for me.

Other New Testament teaching on giving includes the following:

1. We are to give regularly, "on the first day of the week" (l Corinthians 16:2).

2. We are to give as God has prospered us (l Corinthians 16:2).

3. We are to give cheerfully (2 Corinthians 9:7).

4. We are to give generously (Romans 12:8).

41

5. We are to give what we can without making a big ado about it (Matthew 6:3).

How then does this New Testament teaching relate to tithing?

Tithing is a good place to start. Most people can tithe. Countless people who have stepped out on faith and given a tithe of their income have found that God blessed them just as Malachi promised.

The New Testament does not emphasize percentages. Giving is a joyous response to the love of God, and tithing is the beginning. Many people can give more than 10%. And that includes senior citizens who have pensions, Social Security, savings, debt-free homes, senior discounts and fewer responsibilities. The challenge for those who may have more disposable income than ever before is to give a larger part of it to the Lord.

We understand also that it is too much to expect some people with limited means to tithe or to give very much at all. God has a special love for these folks and blesses them for whatever they may be able to give.

Some people who are retired or unemployed give generously by volunteering their help for some part of the Lord's work. If you think of their services as being worth six dollars an hour, it's easy to see that their contributions are substantial.

Giving, however it is done, is the key to joyful living. Our God is a giving God — that is His nature. And if we are to share in His life, we must also be givers.

Two bodies of water in the Holy Land provide a great natural illustration of this principle. The Sea of Galilee has delightful, clear water. Multitudes of fish live in this sea on which Jesus once walked. Travelers slake their thirst with its refreshing waters. Less than 100 miles south is another large body of water. The Dead Sea contains not a single fish and no one would think of drinking its salty water.

What is the difference? The Sea of Galilee receives and gives — its waters are always flowing. The Dead Sea receives water and it stays there. The only escape for its waters is by evaporation.

Joyous, healthy people are receiving and giving. That's what Jesus was teaching us when He said: "It is more blessed to give than to receive" (Acts 20:35).

22.
"I READ A LOT ABOUT ANGELS THESE DAYS. DOES EACH OF US HAVE A GUARDIAN ANGEL? IF SO, HOW CAN I GET IN TOUCH WITH MINE?"

People are thinking about angels today. *Time* magazine reported that 69% of Americans believe that angels exist, and 46% believe that they have their own guardian angel. Books about angels are on the bestseller lists. One national woman's magazine published an article reporting four different angel appearances and then invited their readers to send in reports of others.

Are angels real?

Hundreds of Scripture passages mention them. Most are related to God's work of salvation. They are especially evident in the saving mission of Christ, at His birth, at His temptation, at Gethsemane, and at the Resurrection and Ascension. And the Bible says that they will accompany Him at His Second Coming.

Peter was delivered from prison by an angel (Acts 12:5-11), and Paul was assured by an angel that he and all on board would survive the coming shipwreck (Acts 27:21-26).

Are there guardian angels for the rest of us?

There is biblical evidence for the belief in guardian angels. Psalm 91:11 gives the assurance, "For he will command his angels concerning you to guard you in all your ways." An echo of this is heard in Psalm 34:7, "The angel of the

Lord encamps around those who fear him, and he delivers them."

The words of Jesus in Matthew 18:10 say that even little children have their angels. "See that you do not look down on one of these little ones. For I tell you that their angels in heaven always see the face of my Father in heaven."

I remember my mother telling me that when I was being prepared for a dangerous mastoid operation, she had a vision of angels surrounding me on the operating table.

Two or three times I have involuntarily turned the wheel of my car in a direction that avoided an accident. I wondered if a guardian angel was at work.

Yes, there are grounds from Scripture and from experience for believing that God sends angels to protect His people.

But we must be cautious. The appearance of angels is a mystery. Why do they come to some people and not to others? It's the same kind of question we ask when some prayers for healing are answered and others are not.

Just because we have never had an experience with angels (and many Christians have not), that does not diminish our relationship with Christ in any way.

We should be careful that our interest in angels does not interfere with our worship of Christ. Paul warns against the worship of angels in Colossians 2:18. In 1 Timothy 2:5, Paul points out that we must focus on Christ. "For there is one God and one mediator between God and men, the man Christ Jesus."

God does use angels and He may use them in our lives for His purposes. But He also works to comfort and guide without angels. Most often, the Lord uses His Word and the promptings of the Holy Spirit.

Let us thank God that people are interested in angels. That may help them sense that the supernatural is real, that God reigns, and that He is in charge of His universe.

To get in touch with your guardian angel, here is a prayer for you, "Lord, I am open to any blessing You want to bring into my life.

If an angel never comes into your life, continue to rest upon the promise that nothing can separate you from the love of God in Christ Jesus.

23.
"IT BOTHERS ME THAT SOME PEOPLE WHO MAKE NO PROFESSION OF CHRISTIAN FAITH ARE NICER THAN MANY OF MY CHRISTIAN FRIENDS."

That is troubling. People who make no profession of faith — a boss, a co-worker, a neighbor — seem unselfish and so easy to get along with. And some people in the church are just the opposite. It makes you wonder about the application of the verse: "Therefore, if anyone is in Christ, he is a new creation; the old has gone, the new has come!" (2 Corinthians 5:17).

One thing to remember is that we can't draw conclusions based on just a few examples. If a giant computer could give a readout on the quality of life of everyone in and out of the church, I am convinced that we would find that a majority of the loving, dedicated people in the world are those who have committed themselves to Jesus Christ.

But how should we think about those nice pagans and nasty Christians?

We can't be absolutely sure about who is a believer and who isn't. Some people who never made a profession of faith or joined a church may indeed be believers. They are wrong for not letting their faith be known. But their kindness and love may indeed be the work of God in their hearts.

Some non-Christians who act like Christians may be drawing from a heritage of Christian training and Christian role models in their families. Even though these people have not yet committed themselves to Christ, some marks of their Christian background remain.

It is important to remember also, that what we call niceness and nastiness often has a lot to do with a healthy or faulty nervous system which people have inherited.

Some Christians who do not seem to be nice may be a lot nicer than they were before they came to Christ. Becoming a Christian does not automatically remove all problems. The promise of the Bible is that God will help us cope with them. Indeed, some people come to Christ because they sense the problems in their lives and understand that they need help.

We never really know what's going on in another person's heart and life. What comes out as nastiness may be the result of enormous stress. If we were in that person's shoes, we might behave just as badly.

God is the one who understands completely. He is just and fair. The names of His children are written in heaven.

We can be sure of one thing.

We have assurance about our own standing before God. The ground of our assurance is not in fallible people or institutions, but in the Word of God. The clear affirmation of Scripture is: "That if you confess with your mouth, 'Jesus is Lord,' and believe in your heart that God raised him from the dead, you will be saved" (Romans 10:9).

Our hope is in Christ.

PART II

Developing Positive
Thoughts About Yourself

24.
"AT MY AGE, WHAT DO I HAVE TO
LOOK FORWARD TO?"

Two minor characters in the Bible's Christmas stories give us a major message — wonderful events may come late in life.

Luke 2:25-35 tells about Simeon, an elderly man, who quietly waited for God to fulfill His promises to Israel. When he listened to reports of political messiahs and the plans of some to revolt against Rome, he would reply that we must wait for God to speak. He may not send that kind of messiah.

The Holy Spirit answered Simeon's prayers with the assurance that he would not die until he had seen the Lord's Christ. Simeon must have wondered about who he would see. Would the Messiah be among the teachers who expounded on the Hebrew Scriptures in the Temple? Would he be a young man? A middle-aged man?

What a surprise when God directed him to Joseph, Mary, and a tiny baby!

The Lord gave Simeon a message for Mary. This baby, the Lord's Messiah, would cause many in Israel to rise and many others to fall. That was an insight repeated by Jesus in John 9:39, "...For judgment I have come into the world, so that the blind will see and those who see will become blind." When Jesus Christ confronts us, we are never the same. We move closer to God, or we move away from Him.

Simeon said something else that Mary must have remembered until the day Jesus went to the cross. Men would oppose Jesus and she would suffer because of her Son — "a sword will pierce your own soul too" (Luke 2:35).

Another quiet person, Anna, a prophetess, never left the Temple. She spent her time in prayer. She thought about God. She shared her insights with those who would listen. When she saw the baby Jesus, she told all who were waiting for the redemption of Israel (Luke 2:36-38).

In the winter of their lives, these two elderly people experienced God in a new way. They teach us beautiful truths about God's plans for His older children.

1. Simeon and Anna knew the power of prayer. It was not men's opinions or human plans that counted. They knew that we must wait upon the Lord. They experienced God's answers to their prayers.

Some of us may be too old for positions of great responsibility and decision making. But we are not too old to meet God through prayer. Late in life, we may experience God's hand in our lives in new and unique ways. Some have decided to major in exploring the power of intercessory prayer during their retirement. They invite people to send them the first names of friends who need prayer.

As we pray, we will rejoice at answered prayers, and we will leave the mystery of unanswered prayers with the Lord. One man prayed for the conversion of seven persons. Before he died, three of them had come to Christ. The other four came to know the Lord after his death.

2. Simeon and Anna surely influenced the lives of many before their deaths. A solemn responsibility of the elderly in Israel was to remind the young of God's mighty acts in their history. The elderly encouraged young people to be faithful to God.

That is a ministry for older people today. One man had the habit of writing uplifting letters to friends. Fifteen years after he wrote one of those letters, he received a note from the widow of the man who had received the letter. She wrote, "My husband kept an envelope for years that was marked, 'for a rainy day.' In that envelope were a few items which he often read and reread for his own encouragement. Your note was one of these, and I thought you would like to have it."

3. The great lesson from the lives of Simeon and Anna is that dreams can be realized late in life. The greatest events in our lives may be ahead. When he was in his seventies, a pastor told me, "I am the pastor of a small church where I am seeing greater results than I saw in larger churches I served years ago."

Should that surprise us? This pastor had a keen mind. He counseled people with the benefit of decades of experience. He believed in a God who speaks through young and old.

Simeon's last words were: "Sovereign Lord, as you have promised, you now dismiss your servant in peace. For my eyes have seen your salvation, which you have prepared in the sight of all people, a light for revelation to the Gentiles and for glory to your people Israel" (Luke 2:29-32). These words have been set to music, often entitled, "Nunc Dimittis." Whether sung or spoken, the stories of these older people provide music to our ears.

God does beautiful things in the lives of His older children.

25.
"IT'S NO FUN BEING OLD. I FEEL THAT NO ONE TAKES ME SERIOUSLY ANYMORE."

A feisty friend of ours wrote on her Christmas card, "The 'golden' years are for the birds. They should call them the 'zinc' years because that rhymes with stink."

No question about it, there are liabilities to old age and one of them is that many people no longer take us seriously.

Several decades ago, a young attractive author made herself up as a heavier woman in her sixties. Then she moved about, making the same contacts she was accustomed to, and took notes. The reactions of people were so dramatically different that she thought it worth writing a book about them.

Apart from age, it is surprising how people discriminate on the basis of physical attractiveness. Recently, a segment on a TV documentary explored the different reactions to attractive and ordinary people. When two women were stranded on a highway, the pretty woman had many offers for help, while the ordinary young woman was ignored. Two young men, one handsome and one not handsome at all, presented resumes with equivalent qualifications. The handsome guy scored each time. Even youngsters seem biased. When two young teachers taught the same class of eight-year-olds, the only variable was physical attractiveness. The kids thought the attractive woman was the better teacher.

It's galling to be rebuffed when we try to establish new relationships. It can be devastating when our work is no longer considered because we are not personally attractive.

If you feel like screaming, "Life isn't fair," go ahead and do it!

But let us also consider these points.

We are still in the land of the living. Some of our contemporaries are not. I can take a deep breath of fresh air every morning, relish a good breakfast, hug my grandchildren, enjoy a concert or football game. I can do these things today, tomorrow and perhaps for some years to come.

And, if I really want to, I can probably find remunerative work. I'll never be invited to be a TV anchor. Probably the day of power lunches with attractive young executives is over. But not every one discriminates on the basis of age — there are establishments which engage older people. In most large cities there are employment agencies that specialize in placing seniors in temporary work. They say that their clients prefer older workers.

If I can find 20, 30, or more hours a week of remunerative employment, and I probably can, I can just forget about the people who don't want me. There are still some people who appreciate what I can do.

Best of all, if we have a minimum of financial security, we have choices. We can arrange for the blend of work and leisure that we prefer. We can say, "No I don't have time this week to work. But thank you, and call again when you need someone." Or, "Thanks for calling, but that just isn't my thing." For the first time in our lives, some of us can reserve our time and energies for the things God has gifted us to do.

It may be worth analyzing what makes it difficult for us to be taken seriously. Do we talk too much? Are we critical of everything new? Is our conversation laced with references to the Great Depression and the Second World War? Let's listen more, let's put ourselves in the places of younger people and try to understand life from their perspective.

Let us initiate new friendships with people who need a friend and repair some older relationships.

We can enjoy life more, because we see it from a broader perspective. We have a better handle on what is important and what is not. We have learned how to savor the joys of a happy, warm experience.

Now, we have time to reflect more on God's revelation to us, to ponder the words of John, "Now this is eternal life: that they may know you, the only true God, and Jesus Christ, whom you have sent" (John 17:3).

The later years may be golden after all.

26.
"I WISH THAT I'D HAD MORE FUN IN LIFE ."

Well, beginning today, let's have more fun.

I had an aunt whose hobby was collecting jokes and telling them to everyone she met. She died at age 93. When I called her I tried to have a new story to tell her. Aunt Peggy even entertained the doctors and nurses in the operating room for five minutes before her surgery.

God wants us to laugh, he wants us to enjoy life. He created a world for us to manage, and He wants us to be happy as we do it. People who order their lives according to God's plans are the best qualified to find the joy He intended for us.

Jesus said: "... I am come that they may have life, and have it to the full" (John 10:10). And there is evidence that Jesus enjoyed life. He attended a wedding and made new wine. He accepted the hospitality of friends. He loved to be around children. His parables indicate that he was a keen observer of nature, and Bible students have detected playful elements in some of his remarks.

Why not try some new things that will bring you joy?

Take a walk in the woods. Observe the evidences of new life.

Play with a child. Children are sure that the world is full of remarkable and exciting things to see and do. Let us learn from them.

When you have a choice, drive on the scenic route.

Visit some place in your city you've never seen before — a museum, historic site, a company that gives tours.

When the circus comes to town, go with your grandkids or some other child.

When friends are coming over for an evening, rent a funny video.

Sit down in an empty church for a few minutes. Open your mind. Perhaps God will tell you something.

Call a friend you haven't seen for a long time and say some encouraging words.

And think of a good story that makes people laugh without putting anyone down.

One aging person had these reflections:

"If I had my life to live over again, I'd dare to make more mistakes next time. I would relax. I would limber up. I would be sillier than I have been this trip.

"I would climb more mountains, swim more rivers, and watch more sunsets. I would do more walking and looking. I would eat more ice cream and less beans. I would have more actual troubles and fewer imaginary ones.

"If I had my life to live again, I would start barefooted in the spring and stay that way late in the fall. I would play more. I would ride on more merry-go-rounds. I'd pick more daisies."

Forget the past, put the future out of your mind. Determine that today you are going to have fun.

It's not too late to make changes.

Let's pick more daisies.

27.
"I LOOK AT SOME PEOPLE AND THINK, EVERYTHING YOU TOUCH SEEMS TO TURN TO GOLD. I'M AFRAID THAT I'VE BATTED LESS THAN .500."

The best major league ball players, even those of Hall of Fame caliber, batted much less than .500. Babe Ruth struck out many more times than he hit home runs.

In graduate school I had the humiliating experience of failing a course. I couldn't believe it. It had never happened before and I thought that it would never happen.

The grade was based on two short essays handed in at the end of the course. I talked with the professor about the failing grade, but even after that conversation, I wasn't sure what had gone wrong.

That experience changed my teaching style. I resolved to do several things:

1. To make the goals and expectations of the course crystal clear to my students.

2. To always ask myself if it was my fault that my students weren't making the progress I expected.

3. To do enough preliminary testing so that students could understand what had to change before the final examination.

That failed course helped students in many classes that I taught in Africa and the United States. It influenced my teaching more than many of the courses in which I received As and Bs.

God teaches us that He is using all of the experiences in our lives for His glory, for our good and for the good of others. The Apostle Paul tells us: "And we know that in all things God works for the good of those who love him, who have been called according to his purpose" (Romans 8:28).

This promise is made to people who love the Lord. A person in rebellion against God cannot expect that the events of his life will ultimately become a blessing. But everything that happens in the lives of God's children will be used in some way for His glory and for their good. The failures, the frustrations and the afflictions we have experienced make us better men and women. Even the sinful experiences that God has forgiven may be used to help others. As he pleaded for forgiveness, David promised God: "Then I will teach transgressors your ways, and sinners will turn back to you" (Psalm 51:13).

In His perfect love and wisdom, God is working for our good.

He doesn't waste anything.

Many wise people have concluded that they learned more from painful experiences than from happy ones. The sad events deepened their spiritual lives and gave them wisdom to face other challenges.

Knowing that God is working in our lives, there is a sense in which we can say that everything we touch *does* turn to gold.

28.
"I HEAR A LOT ABOUT TIME MANAGEMENT. NOW THAT I'M RETIRED, THAT PROBABLY DOESN'T MATTER ANY MORE."

It's more important than ever. If you are retired, you have more time at your disposal than ever before. To use that time well requires planning and discipline.

One temptation is to aimlessly shop or watch television. Another is to let other people fill up your time with so-so activities, offering the message, spoken or unspoken, "Now that you are retired you have plenty of time. You can do this or that."

Retired persons have the same gifts and talents from God that they had during their most active years, plus a great deal of experience. Some people were never able to use those gifts to their maximum in the jobs they held. Now there is another opportunity. If you use your gifts well, your greatest contribution to the Lord and to others may come during your retirement years.

Here are some ways to think about managing your time:

1. Set measurable goals that you want to accomplish within a specific period of time. At the end of that time, evaluate the progress. You may have to make some adjustments. But you are making yourself accountable. You are not just drifting.

In his autobiography, Lee Iacocca tells that when he was at both Ford and Chrysler, he asked every person in management to tell his superior some specific things that he wanted to accomplish during the next three months. They wrote it down. Three months later they discussed how the goals had been met, or, if necessary, what went wrong. It improved performance.

These might be some of your personal goals:

To contact by letter or phone several members of your extended family.

To lose 30 pounds (OK, let's make it 15).

To read the Old Testament.

To clean the junk out of your house.

To take at least one course that will stretch you intellectually.

To teach a course that will enable you to pass on to others some things you have learned.

To volunteer for a job in your church or community that you never had time to do.

Whatever your goals, write them down and tell someone else about them. That makes you accountable.

2. Another technique is to make a list of the things you want to do on a certain day or during a certain week. Then assign priorities. What should be done first, second, and what can wait? Begin with the first item on the list. Work at it until your discretionary time runs out. Then, when you have more time for that project, resume work. Keep on until it is done. Then take on the second project. It works!

3. Another way to think about time management is to consider the little blocks of time in your day — ten, fifteen minute segments when you are not completely engaged. Waiting for the bus, riding in the back of someone's car, waiting for your grandchild whose rehearsal lasted longer than you thought. Can you plan for reading, writing, crocheting, during those tiny segments of time?

One of the most important books of the 19th century was Harriet Beecher Stowe's *Uncle Tom's Cabin*. It galvanized the opposition to slavery and gave impetus to the abolition movement. Mrs. Stowe managed a home with six children. She wrote the first draft of that book on sheets of butcher paper as the evening meal cooked on the stove.

Paul had a sense of urgency about his mission in life, "...making the most of every opportunity, because the days are evil," (Ephesians 5:16), and "...the time is short" (1 Corinthians 7:29).

You have as much time as any billionaire. You have as much time as the President of the United States. You have 24 hours, 1,440 minutes every day. When the day is over, that time has gone forever.

If you are retired, you have more discretion over that time than ever. Manage it well.

29.
"I GET SO DEPRESSED. I WISH THAT I COULD DEAL BETTER WITH THESE TERRIBLE FEELINGS."

One of the Bible's classic cases of depression appears in the life of the prophet, Elijah. God had just given Elijah a great demonstration of his power as He sent down fire from heaven in response to Elijah's prayer. Now Queen Jezebel vowed to kill him. Elijah spent a day running away and then, discouraged, he sat down under a tree and asked to die.

You can read about the four steps in God's therapy in 1 Kings 19.

1. After Elijah had slept a while, the Lord sent someone to give him food (vs. 5-8). Our bodies are often part of the problem in depression. When we rest, when we eat good food, life becomes bearable. Our problems begin to look manageable.

2. Then the Lord gave Elijah some facts (vs. 18). He helped him check out his arithmetic. He told Elijah that he wasn't alone. There were seven thousand faithful people in Israel who had not bowed to Baal.

God may directly give us new insights, but he often sends friends who can help us see our problems from a different perspective. We need these friends to check out our arithmetic and other elements in our situation.

3. The Lord gave Elijah a demonstration of his power, a powerful wind, an earthquake and then a fire. But, after all the noise there was a still small voice or a gentle whisper (vs. 11-13). The point was that God works more often in quiet ways than in the occasional spectacular event. When we are depressed about problems, let us remember that we have a great God who has promised to never leave us.

4. Finally, the Lord gave Elijah something to do. He instructed him to anoint two kings and he told him to get on with the training of his successor, Elisha (vs. 15-17). We shouldn't wait for our feelings to change. We can do things we know we should do even though we don't feel like doing them. As we act, our feelings will change.

Several years ago, *Decision* magazine carried the story of a young English teacher who wrote of a day when he felt very depressed. He decided that he would go out for a drive. Before long he saw a young man trying to hitch a ride. He didn't want a passenger. He just wanted to be alone.

But it was raining and the teacher decided to pick him up. He thought: "I'll give him a ride, I won't have to say much. We will sit in silence. He'll escape the rain. I can still be alone."

There was a Bible in the car and the hitchhiker asked: "Do you believe what's in that book?"

The English teacher knew then that he might have to say something about his faith, but he didn't feel like telling him of victory in Jesus, when he didn't feel victorious himself. "Why," he asked himself, "did the Lord have to send this fellow to me? Why couldn't he send him to a victorious Christian?"

The hitchhiker began to talk about his torment and his dependence on drugs. And the English teacher, as best he could, told him about Christ, His power and His offer of salvation, everything he knew which would help the hitchhiker.

The teacher said: "As I talked, something amazing began to happen. I began to feel marvelously comforted myself. As I was forced to explain my newly espoused faith, I became confident that God could handle not only this young man's problems but my own as well. I began to feel the joy of the Lord."

He concluded: "Angels in heaven rejoiced for that young man, but I am sure that the spiritual celebration went beyond that. Somewhere an angel was also rejoicing for me. I had experienced the healing power of Christ."

30.
"I FEEL THAT THIS IS GOING TO BE MY LAST YEAR, I'M NO GOOD TO ANYONE ANYMORE."

If this is going to be your last year, why not make it one of your best?

We can't do much about national and international events. We don't have a lot of control over what people might do or say to us. But we can make decisions about how we will react to them. We can choose what we want to think about. We can order our private world.

The book of Philippians is a hope-filled book, written by the Apostle Paul at a time when he thought that he might have less than a year to live. The key to his outlook is expressed in Philippians 1:21, "For to me, to live is Christ and to die is gain."

Paul could say, "Either way I win, I'm ready to enjoy eternity with Christ, but if God gives me a few more years, I want to visit you friends in Philippi. I want to go to Spain." As uncertain as his future was, he was dreaming, he was setting goals.

Why not set some goals this year?

How about making a list of the people you know who are having a hard time? Contact each of them by phone or letter every couple of months and ask about how they are doing, and tell them that you are praying for them.

Or what about writing a letter to people who have made a difference in your life? Let them know how much you have appreciated them. You'll make their day. You will be echoing Paul's words, "I thank my God every time I remember you " (Philippians 1:3).

Whatever your goal, if you keep your mind on the good things you want to accomplish, God will help you seize opportunities to make those things come true.

In prison, Paul determined that he was going to be a blessing to every person who crossed his path. We get hints of how that happened when he told us that the whole palace guard knew why he was there. He sent greetings from the "saints in Caesar's household" (Philippians 4:22). Apparently he was telling everybody the Good News that Christ was alive and could make a difference in their lives. And some believed him.

Like Paul, we can make vows to ourselves and to God that everyone who crosses our path will know that we love God and that we love them. The health care worker, the repairman — send them away with an upbeat word. If a person does a good job, tell him so. If you can put in a good word for Christ, try to do that.

As Paul waited in prison, he came to understand God's great plan of salvation in a more profound way. He talked about "how wide and long and high and deep is the love of Christ" (Ephesians 3:18). He described God's eternal purpose "to bring all things in heaven and on earth together under one head, even Christ" (Ephesians 1:10).

This year we can have new adventures in the Word of God. We can experience answers to prayer. We can deepen our understanding of God's ways to men and women.

You can be refreshed and instructed by reading books that describe how God is working in people's lives. Such a book is *Rise and Walk,* written by former New York Jets lineman, Dennis Byrd. He thought he might be paralyzed for life from a game injury, but he found that God responded in a beautiful way to his prayers. Or, you may want to go deeper in the ways of God to men and women in a profound little book, *Where Is God When It Hurts,* by Philip Yancey.

If you begin acting like Paul, you will dream and learn. You will make a difference in people's lives. Your last year may be one of your best.

The truth is you may not want to die this year, and maybe God will decide that you shouldn't!

31.
"I HAVE SO MANY THINGS I WANT TO DO, AND I FEEL THAT TIME IS GETTING SHORT."

When I think of things still to be accomplished I remember the words of Paul written during his last imprisonment in Rome, "Come before winter."

In the closing passage of 2 Timothy, Paul says that the time of his death is at hand. He asks Timothy to bring his books and his cloak. Most of all he wanted to see Timothy himself. He tells him, "Do thy diligence to come before winter " (2 Timothy 4:21 KJV).

Why winter?

The Mediterranean was not navigable during several winter months. If Timothy waits too long, the last boat will have left and he must wait until spring.

We would like to think that Timothy hastened to the port, sailed for Rome and had a blessed time of fellowship with Paul. In the next weeks perhaps he helped Paul write letters, discussed plans for new churches, and then, possibly, accompanied Paul to his execution.

Another scenario is that Timothy waited. He missed the last boat and waited until spring. When he arrived in Rome he heard the sad news that Paul had been put to death. Perhaps some Christian passed on Paul's last words: "Give my love to Timothy, my beloved son."

We'll never know the real end of this story. But Paul's words challenge us, "Come before winter."

There are days of opportunity, but they pass.

Probably we will see several more winters, but we will feel better if some affairs are cared for before this one passes.

One technique to handle this is to make a list of the things you know need to be done. Set a reasonable time period for their completion. Then begin with the first, go on to the second, and continue until the list is completed. These might be some of the things you should accomplish:

A will drawn up to properly distribute your assets.

A living will that describes the level of medical care that you want when it is determined that your death is near.

A reunion with close friends.

An expression of appreciation to people who meant a great deal to your life.

Telling some people that you love them.

In the same letter to Timothy, Paul wrote these words, "I have fought the good fight, I have finished the race, I have kept the faith" (2 Timothy 4:7).

Paul had the satisfaction of knowing that he had completed his mission. He was ready to meet the Lord.

His call to Timothy is a message to us all.

Come before winter!

32.
"I READ A LOT ABOUT SETTING GOALS AND SEEING RESULTS. THAT IS ALL WELL AND GOOD FOR WORKING PEOPLE. I'M CONFINED TO A RETIREMENT HOME."

Your mission in life didn't stop with your retirement and it didn't end when you entered a retirement community or nursing home. Wherever you live, you can serve God and bless others. Here are some goals you might consider:

In a nursing home community, there are nurses, aides, food service workers, and maintenance people. When you see someone doing a good job, why not tell her so? You might be amazed at what a pick-up that can be to a worker. Don't compliment a person unless she is doing a good job.

But if she is, say something like, "You make this community a better place for us all." Why not set a goal to do this at least once a week?

You could write out a list of the people in your world — family, friends, and people you think about who have special needs. Then pray for them each day. Some people find it useful to list their prayer requests in a notebook and write the date when an answer comes. The Bible teaches us, "The prayer of a righteous man is powerful and effective" (James 5:16).

Have you ever read the Bible through? Why not plan to systematically read it? Some parts of both Testaments are difficult to understand, but get what you can from the readings. If you read from a study Bible, you will find that the notes at the bottom of each page will answer many questions. The reading of a psalm will almost always provide a spiritual blessing.

Why learn new Bible truths at an advanced age? One good reason is that when we pass from this life, Christians enter the presence of God. The more we learn about God now, the better equipped we will be to enjoy heaven.

Who knows? In realizing these goals you might make more spiritual progress in a year in that nursing home than you did during the last twenty years.

Do you have a phone? Why not make it a goal to regularly call some people with whom you no longer have contact? You might want to call a few people every couple of weeks, some every two or three months, others just once a year. Make the calls short, ask about what is going on in their lives and plan to say something encouraging. If you get the voice mail, record an encouraging message. After making a few of these calls, you won't feel lonely.

How about keeping a journal, noting something new that you observe each day in your home? Include in this journal your reactions to some of the current events you hear about.

Why not pick out a person who has few visitors and seems lonely? Become her special friend. Listen to her, introduce your visitors to her. Think of something uplifting to say each day. You can't do that for everyone, but you can do it for one person.

Are there classes in handcrafts? Could you make some things that might be given as Christmas presents?

Are there special jobs you might undertake? Could you become the person in charge of ordering inspiring literature that might be placed in a literature rack or given to people with special needs? A visiting chaplain or pastor could help you get started on such a project.

Most people in retirement communities or nursing homes can set goals and see results. God has given you a mission to light a lamp wherever you are.

33.
"I'M ATTENDING MORE FUNERALS THESE DAYS. YET, I STILL FEEL AWKWARD ABOUT SAYING SOMETHING HELPFUL TO THE LOVED ONES OF THE DECEASED PERSON."

The first thing to remember is that just being there tells the family that we cared. The time and effort taken to arrive at the viewing or the funeral makes a statement more powerful than the words we speak.

But what are good things to say and what should be avoided?

Remarking about how beautiful the corpse looks is not helpful. Death is ugly, it is the end of some beautiful relationships here on earth. A well-prepared corpse does not change that.

Let us be careful about making statements about the will of God. That is a profound subject and glib remarks spoken about God's will may not help the bereaved.

Let us also beware of statements such as: "At least he didn't suffer," or "at least her children are grown." Death, under the best conditions, involves separation and that is sad.

Then, what should we say?

Why not share your own feelings about what the deceased person meant in your life?

"You know Harry helped me get started with the company. I don't know whether I could have made it without him."

"Adelia was like a second mom to me."

"I will never forget the time Rachel brought cooked meals to our home when both of my kids were sick."

If you can elaborate on some special quality or accomplishment in the person's life, that will hearten the bereaved person and honor the memory of the deceased.

A friend told me how a visitor remarked at her father's casket about how much he loved to walk, and then shared some experiences he remembered about that.

Without preaching, we can say a few words that point to our Christian hope.

"We're praying for you, Jim. We know that God is going to bring you through this."

"It's so good to know that Bill is with the Lord."

"Jean's suffering is over and we thank God for that."

Sometimes a family member or friend is asked to say a few words at the funeral. Why not share an incident that demonstrates his faith and character?

When my brother spoke at my aunt's funeral, he told a story that had often made us smile. Aunt Anna gave to anyone who said he was hungry. One day, a beggar came to the door and she was about to reach for her pocketbook when she thought about how the money might be spent. So she asked, "You don't drink, do you?" He quickly replied,

"Lady, I'll take a drink any time." My aunt's response to that was, "Then you're not getting my money."

The hearers smiled. A little story that made a point about Aunt Anna's life — compassion, but also strong convictions.

Don't be afraid to let people smile or even laugh. We are celebrating the life of our friend and that included humor as well as sadness, happy times as well as sad ones.

To help those who are grieving, let us celebrate the Christian hope, and let us celebrate a life well-lived.

34.
"SOME PEOPLE ARE GREAT ENCOURAGERS, I WISH I COULD BE ONE OF THEM."

You can be!

Barnabas, Paul's companion on his first missionary journey, wasn't in the first line of apostles, but he had the gift of encouraging others. He encouraged Paul when he needed an introduction to the Christian community.

When Paul arrived in Jerusalem after his conversion, some believers were reluctant to accept him. They couldn't believe that the man who had worked havoc in the Church had now made a 180 degree turn in his life. Barnabas assured them that God had made a permanent change in Paul.

I can imagine that one evening the two men, arm in arm, entered a home where a group of believers had gathered. Barnabas said: "Friends, this is brother Saul. He has met the Lord and has become a new man. Brother Saul is an example of how God is working in our midst. He is one of us now."

Barnabas was an optimist. He believed that God could change people.

Becoming an encourager means taking a risk. If Paul had failed, Barnabas would have heard those famous words: "I told you so."

Giving encouragement means taking time to listen to someone. It involves getting into his world and understanding his feelings.

A young man named Will Wright, who serves now as a mechanic with Mission Aviation Fellowship in Africa, experienced a turning point in his life when he had an accident on a tractor. He lost the fingers on his left hand. That accident eventually propelled him back to school, and later to good jobs with substantial companies. Finally, God led Will to become a mechanic in Africa.

Will said that a key person during those early days after his accident was the teacher of his college and career class. He talked a lot with her. She listened and encouraged him with words like, "Will, I can see a great change in you since that accident."

The beautiful thing about encouraging another person is that we share in that person's success. Like spraying perfume in a room, it's hard not to get some on yourself.

I have a book in my library entitled *Hospitality With Confidence—Opening Your Home and Heart, Efficiently, Gracefully and Lovingly,* by Grace Pittman. In her introduction she wrote these words: "I need to say a special thanks to Dr. Willard Scofield for getting me started on this project and asking about it often enough to keep me motivated."

That introduction encouraged me. I had a part in Grace Pittman's work.

The teacher of that college and career class had something to do with Will Wright's work in Africa.

Barnabas shared in the ministry of Paul, the greatest of all the apostles.

Encouragers always win!

35.
"BUT SOMETIMES I JUST DON'T KNOW WHAT TO SAY TO ENCOURAGE PEOPLE."

Here are some simple suggestions:

Encouragement involves listening. It's making a long distance phone call to someone who is unemployed, to ask about his progress, and to assure him that you are praying for him.

Encouragement must be sincere. You shouldn't build a person up with words that you don't really believe yourself.

Encouragement should be specific. Pastors like to hear parishioners tell them that their sermons have been helpful. If you mention some specific point that helped you, it's even better.

One sentence, spoken sincerely and lovingly, can work wonders.

These are some things you might say to adults:

"I loved your dinner, I've never tasted a souffle like that before."

"I'm glad you're in our group."

"I really appreciated your listening to me today."

"You've got so much to offer. I know you're going to find another job."

"You've tried hard and stuck with it. I admire that."

"Those mission display tables were nicely done. I appreciate all the work you did."

"It takes a while to learn to do this. You're doing fine."

Here are some things you might say to children:

"I liked the way you shared your toys with Jimmy."

"You're my special friend. I like being with you."

"You're really improving."

"A boy who can build something like that could be an

engineer some day."

The words you say may be remembered for decades.

I'm certain that Simon Peter never forgot these words of Jesus: "I will make you fishers of men" (Matthew 4:19).

Several decades later, I still remember the words of the teacher who told me that she appreciated my hard work, and of another who predicted success for me. I still recall the warm, reassuring letter an 18-year-old friend wrote to me after I had to drop out of college because of pneumonia.

Vince Lombardi, the great coach of the Green Bay Packers, disciplined his players, but he also knew how to encourage them. One day he chided a guard named Jerry Kramer for missing several blocks during practice. Later, in the locker room, Lombardi put his hand on Kramer's shoulder and said one sentence, "One of these days, you're going to be one of the best guards in the NFL."

Jerry Rramer said that he carried that image of himself throughout his career, a career that led to the Hall of Fame and membership on the NFL's all 50-year team.

Encouraging words last a long time!

36.
"WHEN PEOPLE ASK QUESTIONS ABOUT MY FINANCIAL SITUATION, I BECOME UNEASY."

One day, a man called to make an appointment to talk about nursing home insurance. He asked me over the phone, "Do you have more than $30,000 that you want to protect?"

A representative of a company that sells mutual funds and life insurance asked one of his prospects to give him a complete description of her assets. He said that he could serve her best if he could see the total picture.

A couple has been giving money to a college for years. Someone from the development department offered free counsel on estate planning. Offhandedly, he asked what tax bracket the couple was in.

If you feel uneasy about giving details of your financial situation to a person who may be a total stranger, you have a right to be.

If I said that I had more than $30,000, my name could be passed on to mailing lists which target seniors with savings.

The life insurance and mutual fund salesman may be right when he says that he can serve you better if he sees the whole picture. But do you know him well enough to tell him the details of your financial situation? If he is working for a company, he may well push the financial products that give him the best commission.

The development person from a college may represent a good cause. However, if he knows your income level, he may pressure you to give more.

The people noted in these examples may be honest, but they have an agenda. Their livelihood depends on getting you to buy into their financial plans. Some sales people will try to push their prospects to make a commitment immediately.

That is what you should not do. You have every right to say, "I want to think this over."

You should think it over and get other opinions on the subject. It may be wise to buy nursing home insurance. However, consider that only a small percentage of people spend long periods in nursing homes. Does this insurance give any benefits for home health care, if you elect that instead of going to a nursing home?

If you are asked to buy life insurance at a guaranteed premium, you should reflect about whether you need more life insurance. If an older person has no one depending on him, he may not need additional protection.

Before you decide about how much you can save in taxes by giving your money to a worthy institution, you should check out the figures with a lawyer or accountant.

It is true that a financial planner can help you best if he knows your total financial situation. But choose such a planner carefully. Get recommendations from others who have used him. Check out the company he represents. A financial planner should be willing to listen to his client so that he knows her comfort level in taking risks. The planner's program for someone else in your circumstances may not be the one for you.

We also know there are scams. Elderly people are contacted by telephone and talked into financial decisions by fast talking con men. Keep these things in mind:

Never accept any sales pitch made over the phone. Say, "No, thank you," and hang up.

Never give information about your financial situation. High tech thieves have been able to access accounts and make transfers or withdrawals.

Never give your credit card number to someone who calls you on the phone.

Never give your social security number to a caller.

Never give numbers of bank or mutual fund accounts.

Check your statements from banks and investment companies to make sure that your account has not been accessed by an unauthorized person.

Is this being paranoid? No, we need to keep our guard up.

Is there a Bible verse that addresses this subject? Proverbs 14:15 says it well: "A simple man believes anything, but a prudent man gives thought to his steps."

Remember, you are in charge of your life. You have the right to keep your business to yourself. You have the right to say, "I want to think this over."

37.
"I STILL WORRY ABOUT FINANCES. I WONDER WHETHER MY MONEY WILL HOLD OUT."

That concern is expressed in many ways.

"What if I have to go into a nursing home?"

"Will there be anything to leave to my children?"

"I've never taken charity before, I hope I don't have to take it at the end of my life."

One way to look at this is to ask how many people we have known who have died without adequate food, shelter, and medical care. The answer is probably, "Very few, if any."

One of the many promises God gives to His children is found in Psalm 121:8, "The Lord will watch over your coming and going both now and forevermore."

Whether they have a little or a lot, older people could profit from expert financial counseling about arranging their resources for the closing years of their lives. Such help might be found through a local senior citizens group.

Financial counselors might point out one of these strategies: If your home is paid for, you might get a home equity loan which you could use for income. Do you have a life insurance policy? Life insurance is purchased for other people, children, or a spouse. If those persons are no longer at risk in the event of your death, you may not need as much. You could cash in the policy, putting aside enough for burial expenses, and the rest could be paid to you in monthly installments. If you have mutual funds, you can ask for a monthly check from these assets. The principal sum and your life expectancy would determine the size of the monthly payments.

Some people worry about leaving something to their children. That is nice to do if you can, but your first consideration is your own needs. You've made your major contribution to your children in raising and educating them.

If one really becomes poor in old age, there are numerous safety nets that provide income and services at low cost. Every one knows about Social Security, but there is also Social Security Supplemental Income for seniors who are poor. In recent years, that payment has been more than $400 monthly to single persons and $600 to couples who meet a means test.

Poor senior citizens are eligible for food stamps. There is Medicaid for those whose incomes do not permit them to pay their medical bills and nursing home costs. Other services include subsidized housing, home delivered meals, aid for utility bills, home maintenance, and many more.

If you hate the thought of taking charity, remember that you have paid taxes all of your life. Some of your tax money is used as a safety net for needy people. It's something like insurance. You've paid for the protection and it's there if you need it.

Some strategies for handling finances in senior years have moral implications. What do you think of the following?

Giving away resources to children to avoid paying for medical expenses or nursing home costs at the end of your life.

Paper divorces to hold on to assets that might have to be used for the nursing home care of a spouse.

Seniors who live together because of Social Security or pension advantages that might be reduced if they married.

To be sure, some of these issues are complicated. Blame can be placed on the government for making laws that create such dilemmas. But, when faced with these issues, we must answer the question, "In the light of God's Word, is this right?"

Is it right to enrich our children by transferring the burden of our medical care to taxpayers of this or a future generation?

Is it right to break God's laws about marriage to secure a financial advantage?

If we are going to give an account of our lives to the Lord in a few years, let us act so that we will be unashamed of our last moral decisions.

Above all, remember, God does care. His promises are still true, "Delight yourself in the Lord and he will give you the desires of your heart" (Psalm 37:4).

<h2 style="text-align:center">38.
"I CAN'T STOP WORRYING ABOUT MY SON'S JOB AND MY DAUGHTER'S MARRIAGE. I'M ALWAYS WORRYING ABOUT GETTING CANCER."</h2>

Early in this century, Sir William Osler, one of the most famous physicians of his era and the founder of the world famous John Hopkins School of Medicine, addressed the students at Yale University. He told them that he had no special brilliance to account for his success. He had been successful, he said, because he had learned to live in day-tight compartments. He used that term because a few months earlier he had crossed the Atlantic on a ship where the captain could press a button and shut off various parts of the ship.

He told the students: "Touch a button and hear, at every level of your life, the iron doors shutting out the past. Touch another and shut off the future, the unborn tomorrows. Then you are safe — safe for today."

Jesus said in Matthew 6:34, "Therefore do not worry about tomorrow, for tomorrow will worry about itself. Each day has enough trouble of its own." Some readers have been confused by this verse, because the King James Version says, "Take therefore no thought for the morrow."

It is not that we should never think about tomorrow or that we never plan for the future. But Jesus taught that we are not to worry about the future. The best way to prepare for tomorrow is to concentrate all of our energies and enthusiasm on today.

Other things that Jesus taught about worry include:

1. Worry is appropriate only for the heathen who have no faith in God (Matthew 6:32).

2. The best way to have a worry-free attitude is to focus on God and His kingdom (Matthew 6:33).

3. If God has given us life, we can trust Him to sustain that life (Matthew 6:30).

4. Worry isn't going to add a cubit (18 inches) to your height, or as some believe Jesus meant, an additional period to your life (Matthew 6:27).

5. God gives beauty to a short lived flower and He can do the same to our lives (Matthew 6:28,29).

One man, after hearing a message on worry at church, went home and wrote all of the things he had worried about on tiny slips of paper. He felt a sense of disgust when he realized that most of his fears never happened. Others, that had some reality, he knew he could handle. He gathered up all of these slips of paper and threw them into a waste basket.

A third group of worries represented a few concerns that would normally give him emotional stress. Of these he said, "The Lord and I can take care of these things."

Every morning when you rise, repeat two verses that will change your life.

"This is the day the Lord has made; let us rejoice and be glad in it" (Psalm 118:24).

"I can do all things through Christ who strengthens me" (Philippians 4:13 NKJV).

You can enjoy today as much as a man or woman who is thirty years younger.

You can do your work and enjoy it.

You can tell some people in your world that you love them.

And you can leave your tomorrows to God.

39.
"WHEN I TALK, NOBODY SEEMS TO BE LISTENING. THAT MAKES ME FEEL SAD AND ALONE."

The reason may be that some older people have lost the art of listening.

That was the conclusion of one university study. The researchers determined that it wasn't because of physical handicaps. Older people listen less because they have lost their curiosity.

They think they've heard it all before. They tend to be dogmatic and are unwilling to consider other viewpoints.

When some older people do seem to listen, they remain in their own world with their own thoughts, waiting to chime in with an opinion of their own.

We can help change that!

Why not consider how you can become a creative listener?

It is mind boggling to realize that God listens to our prayers. David says in Psalm 4:3: "Know that the Lord has set apart the godly for himself; the Lord will hear when I call to him."

Think of it! God listens to me! One person out of the five billion who inhabit this planet. He knows that I am a unique individual, unlike any of His other creatures. He doesn't say, "I've heard it all before."

Just as our God does, we can provide a beautiful experience for someone else by listening. And in giving that gift, we enrich our own life.

Here are some things to remember about creative listening:

1. Maintain eye contact with the person who is speaking.

2. Encourage her to talk by asking questions and then saying things like: "I see" or "I understand."

3. An important part of the listening process is mirroring back what has been said. Something like: "You felt that John wasn't being fair in telling all his friends and leaving you out."

4. Ask questions about things that are not clear. Your question may help to clear the matter in the speaker's own mind.

5. Give your friend an opportunity to explore her feelings by asking things like, "How would you feel if Adele invited you to come back to their group?"

6. You may have some relevant experience or information to share. Try to say something that really relates to the problem your friend has been talking about.

7. If a real concern has been presented, you can mention that you will pray about the need. Then, if you ask about it the next time you meet, your friend will know that you really were listening.

Does this guarantee that others will listen to you? Not necessarily. But in listening creatively, you have entered another person's world. You have given her a chance to speak, to clarify her feelings, and perhaps gain new insights.

You have given her a beautiful gift.

I am a member of a writers' critique group. Six of us meet to listen to each other's writing. Each person has twenty-five minutes to read and have their work discussed. Those twenty-five minutes give me encouragement and ideas about how my work can be improved. But my responsibility is to give my total attention to the work of every other member of the group.

It works.

Let us make a similar contract in our own minds for all of our social gatherings.

I will listen more than I talk.

I will give everyone some time.

I will try to understand.

Don't be surprised if your feelings of sadness and aloneness disappear.

40.
"I FEEL SO LONELY, AND I DON'T KNOW HOW TO OVERCOME IT."

It is lonely when you no longer hear the key in the door that signaled a happy time of conversation with your spouse.

It is lonely when our children no longer need a home-cooked meal and our loving guidance.

It is lonely at family reunions, when you sense that family members are living in a world that is alien to yours.

Some people feel that it's harder to be alone than to be hungry.

We can never bring back the relationships that filled our lives in other days. But we can cope with loneliness.

Have you watched a small child playing by herself, talking, laughing? When one father asked his daughter what was going on, she replied, "Oh, I'm having such a good time with me."

Our solitude becomes enjoyable when we can genuinely accept that we are important to God and that we have creative activities to engage us.

But we also need to move into a community. I was raised in a New York City apartment house where the dwellers, like ships in the night, passed each other in the halls with just a brief nod or a quick hello. But my mother made it a point to talk to people and learn about some of the events in their lives. She learned about the daughters of a lady on the first floor who were Catholic sisters. And on the third floor there was a Jewish family who felt comfortable enough to ask that someone in our family light the lamps on a Friday night when their orthodox father visited. My mother was never alone in that apartment house.

We need to become a part of a community of Christian believers where we will seek not just inspiration, but involvement and responsibility. We should be in a community where we notice when someone is missing and where we are missed.

Our loneliness should prompt us to cultivate a sense of the presence of Christ. It takes only a few minutes to go through a list of prayer requests, but prayer is a time for listening. It's a time to think of great biblical affirmations such as, "Lo I am with you always" (Matthew 28:20 KJV), and "Be still and know that I am God" (Psalm 46:10 KJV).

Prayer may be a time to picture Christ walking with me down the street. When we come to a crossroads, I imagine Him pointing me to the right. It may be a time to picture Him holding my hand as I walk down a flight of stairs.

Some years ago the newspapers reported a power failure in a Salt Lake City hotel that left an elevator between floors in total darkness. Rescue workers, who knew there was a woman in the elevator, called out, "Are you alone down there?"

"I'm by myself," came the reply, "but I am not alone."

She understood and we understand that with Christ we are never alone.

41.

"I WAS DEVASTATED WHEN I WAS EASED OUT OF MY JOB. MY BEST YEARS SEEMED JUST AHEAD OF ME."

Companies all over the U.S., from the smallest to those in the Fortune 500 group, are downsizing, and older workers are often the targets. They cost more in salaries and medical benefits, and some companies think they are not adaptable to new methods.

Does the Bible address such a situation? Yes it does, and the message may be summed up in a couple of sentences. You are a unique child of God who has a special package of spiritual gifts and natural talents. They will remain until you die, and for all we know, perhaps right into eternity.

Nothing can change that. Your circumstances may change, but you are a person of value. You have a mission in life.

Here are more things to think about.

Most older workers who want to work do find something. It may be at lower wages. It may be part-time. It may be a series of temporary jobs. But they do work and any kind of work is better than idleness. Some find a job better than the one they lost.

This is a time to seek help — perhaps consulting a vocational counselor who could give some scientific tests to discover yet unknown abilities and interests. It's possible that the good-paying job you lost was really not the exact fit for you. In later years, you may find something that you enjoy doing more. When you say to yourself, "It's not worth it, I'm too old for vocational counseling," think about how many more years you would like to live and work — five, ten, fifteen. It is worth it.

To do a little self-analysis, think of the activities you perform which make time fly. Think of what has brought you the greatest satisfaction — the things you would do whether you were paid or not.

One of the best books on job searching and career changing is *What Color Is Your Parachute?*, by Richard Nelson Bolles (Ten Speed Press). More than four million copies have been sold and it is updated every year. It will give you ideas and it will warm your heart.

While you are unemployed, it would be wise to join a support group for people like yourself. Some larger churches sponsor such groups. There, you will get information about networking and other resources for finding a job as well as emotional and spiritual support from people who are facing the same problem.

Since you may be required to live on less income, it would be wise to talk to a financial planner. Let him talk to you about taxes, investments, the equity in your home, insurance, Social Security and other pieces in your financial picture.

Think about the possibility of using your training and experience in a business of your own. The federal government's Small Business Administration provides information on this, including ways to finance a small business. Other counseling services can be found in the United Way's listing of helping agencies. The man who painted and papered our home, now about 60, was terminated from a middle management job in his late forties. Working with his wife, he started his home decorating business and today they have more work than they can handle.

Could some of your skills be used in a Christian mission? An organization called "Intercristo" lists hundreds of openings in the United States and overseas. There are probably jobs that match your skills and experience. Some pay a modest salary. For others, one must raise support from the gifts of friends and churches. In recent years, hundreds of people have given a few months to several years in an overseas or home mission that has brought them satisfaction. Many such people have said, "These were the greatest years of my life." The address of Intercristo is P.O. Box 33487, 19303 Freemont Ave. N., Seattle, WA 98133.

Two friends of ours took early retirement and went to Congo to train literacy tutors. They arrived when they were about sixty and continued for several years. Their work was needed and they found great satisfaction in it.

When the question crosses your mind, "Don't you think I'm too old for that?" — always follow that with the affirmation, "Other people have done it and I can too."

More important than anything else is how you think about your unemployment and yourself. If you are bitter, if you think you're finished, that you're too old, that nothing will ever be as good as your former job, that's probably the way it will be.

If you believe that God is going to work in your life and there is something important for you to do, you are likely to encounter opportunities that will make that assumption come true.

You are loved by God. Your premature termination might be the greatest thing that ever happened to you. You may discover, as did the manager of the feast in Cana of Galilee, that the best wine was saved for the last.

42.
"I WISH I WERE YOUNGER. I'D LEARN TO PLAY ONE OF THOSE ELECTRIC ORGANS."

Have you ever slipped into an empty church where the organist was playing stirring music and said to yourself, "What a thrill that must be for her. I'd give anything to be able to play like that"?

You are not too old to have that thrill. Along with the purchase of an electric organ, you can buy a set of lessons which will provide an instructor who will help you learn to play simple music in a few weeks. If you were to look into one of those classes, you would see that a good percentage of the people are seniors. Some senior centers have activities to help seniors develop their musical talents.

Simplified arrangements of all kinds of music have been prepared that anyone can play after a little practice. You can find these easy-to-play compositions in classical music, pop tunes, hymns — just about anything you would want to play.

You don't even need to buy an organ. You can hear yourself playing organ music on a keyboard that you can buy for much less than an electric organ. It would take years to receive the same satisfaction from the piano or some other instrument. The people in a music store can give you details about the different things you can do with a keyboard.

The good news is that people our ages and older can hear themselves playing beautiful music. Millions of people who have only been spectators of art should know that they can become participants. For most of us, there is probably an undiscovered artistic dimension to our personalities. People discover this in a variety of ways.

When she was in her sixties, a friend of ours learned to do oil painting on trays, vases and other objects. This is sometimes called rosemaling. She began learning in an adult education class and developed her skill to the point where she created many beautiful, personalized gifts.

My wife and I once attended classes in calligraphy for several weeks. It was fun. Even though my handwriting is almost indecipherable, I discovered that I could do beautiful writing. I smiled as I imagined my church some day inviting me to do the lettering on Daily Vacation Bible School certificates.

One community education catalog has this list of art-related courses: "the art of embossing, decorating with paint, creative window treatments, cake decorating, needlework, watercolor sampler and woodcarving."

There is evidence today that when children are involved in music and art, that stimulates their brains to work better in other areas such as mathematics. That is probably true for older people as well. Artistic activities may enhance our mental life in ways that we do not yet completely understand.

When we ask the question, "Am I too old for that?" always follow it up with another question, "How old will I be if I don't do it?"

If you are entering retirement, you may well expect two decades or more of life. In fact, during the next ten years, you may have more discretionary time than you had during earlier years when you worked and cared for children.

You can do remarkable things with that time.

Go ahead and begin!

This week!

43.
"I ALWAYS THOUGHT I WOULD LIKE TO EDIT A SMALL MAGAZINE."

All of us have said, "I wonder what it would have been like to ..." The good news is that you may still be able to find out.

To take the illustration of editing a publication, a person could have that experience by preparing a newsletter for her church or another organization in the community. Several journalistic skills such as reporting, writing, editing, interviewing, and designing a layout are part of putting an attractive newsletter together.

Your extended family would probably be grateful if you

prepared a family newsletter that was mailed twice a year. You would call your family members and get news about what is going on in their lives. Such a letter would draw your family together.

Many newsletters are poorly prepared. They could be improved by using more names, discovering interesting stories, using direct quotes and arranging the materials to make reading easier.

Here's another idea. In a church where I served as interim pastor, the people prepared a booklet with short Christmas reflections written by the members — one for each day from December 1 to 25.

One writer remembered the kindness of a neighbor at Christmas in an army camp overseas nearly four decades ago.

A nurse explained why she liked working on Christmas Day in a nursing home. She found special joy in helping lonely seniors experience a warm, meaningful Christmas.

A man described how his son had installed a fluorescent light over his desk. He said that his son thought of his need, spent a substantial amount of money for the light, and took quite a bit of time to install it. The writer concluded, "As I think of my gifts to others, I should consider the needs of the people in my life and make their gifts a personal expression of my love."

You could have a rich experience putting a booklet like that together. You could edit the contributions and interview people who would hesitate to write out a reflection. You would have the challenge of finding illustrations.

Experiences like this would produce the same satisfactions you might have had in editing a small magazine.

Have you ever thought you might have liked to be a counselor? Many communities have a program called "peer counseling" where seniors receive training to counsel other seniors.

If you would like to help people prepare their income taxes, the AARP organization and the IRS train seniors to help other seniors do that.

If you are into computers and using the internet, you could train other seniors to do that in community education programs.

To discover the range of possibilities, talk with people who organize volunteer activities at the United Way or at the Salvation Army. You will discover how your old skills may be used and how you may learn some new ones as well.

God used older people in Bible times. Why shouldn't we expect Him to open new chapters in our lives today?

44.
"IF I EVER LEARN THAT I HAVE A TERMINAL ILLNESS, I WANT TO CONTROL THE TIME I DIE."

A distinction should be made between terminating life and prolonging death. You have the right to opt for minimal medical intervention during the last days of a terminal illness. You may sign a living will that specifies your wish that no "heroic measures" be used to sustain your life when all hope of recovery is gone.

It is important that you discuss your wishes with your family. Even when a living will has been made, doctors will often accede to the wishes of the family if asked to keep a patient on life support equipment.

But ending your life because of the prospect of a painful terminal illness is another matter. Does God want us to do that? Or has He planned experiences for us right to the end?

David seems to have thought so as he wrote the words in Psalm 139:15-16, "My frame was not hidden from you when I was made in the secret place. When I was woven together in the depths of the earth, your eyes saw my unformed body. All the days ordained for me were written in your book before one of them came to be."

When a doctor says you have so much time to live, he is giving you an average. Many people have lived long beyond the average. Others have had remissions, some of which may have been related to prayer. And today doctors have better means of pain control which should alleviate fears.

It could be that God has planned the richest, the most exciting six months or two years for us at the end of our lives.

One man who wondered why God kept him alive was called to court as a witness. He was the only one who could have given the testimony that brought real justice.

People with terminal illnesses have discovered for the first time how much God loves them. They have made the last couple of years a time when they have communicated their faith in a beautiful way.

As death approached, husbands and wives have reported drawing closer together. When speaking of the last two years of her husband's life, one woman said: "We tried to make each day worth living instead of counting how many were left. We took delight in morning coffee, drives in the country, and watching our grandchildren."

If you end your life prematurely, you may lose beautiful moments with the people you love. There may be relationships that need healing. Some people need to hear things you've wanted to say, but never did. Some need to know how much you love them.

Those last weeks may be a time when we shall understand God and the meaning of life more clearly than ever before. It may be a time when we will have a foretaste of the joy that is beyond.

And we will leave with the victorious assurance that

Dietrich Bonhoeffer expressed to the Nazi guards who accompanied him to his execution. With his face shining in joyful expectation he said, "For you it is an end, for me a beginning."

45.
"IF I HAD A SPOUSE WITH ALZHEIMER'S DISEASE, I DON'T THINK I COULD COPE WITH THAT."

Sadly, increasing numbers of people are going to have loved ones with Alzheimer's disease. The frequency of this terrible ailment seems to be increasing. It has been estimated that we will see the time when a fifth of the population over 75 will have Alzheimer's, and perhaps one half of all over 85 will suffer from this disease.

Alzheimer's kills brain cells more quickly than normal. The victim experiences gradual memory loss, a decline in the ability to perform routine tasks, impaired judgment, disorientation, loss of language skills, and eventually, the ability to care for himself. Later, he will not be able to recognize close family members. He will not remember his own name. All the while, the rest of his body may be functioning normally.

If this terrible disease comes into your family, God will give you and others the grace to meet the challenge. You will cope better if you keep some of the following things in mind:

1. When Alzheimer's is suspected, a diagnosis should be sought from a center that specializes in this disease. Some Alzheimer's symptoms are similar to those of diseases which can be treated.

2. The primary care-givers for Alzheimer's patients are often called second victims. If a care-giver is to survive, she must take care of herself. There is a life ahead after the death of the loved one, or after his entry into a nursing home.

3. The whole family should be enlisted to think through the care of the Alzheimer's victim. Are there family members who could substitute for the primary care-giver for a day, or even several hours? Are there friends who would volunteer time for such care?

4. Before the Alzheimer's victim loses touch, legal matters including the granting of power-of-attorney should be cared for.

5. It would be wise to check out nursing homes or Alzheimer's care centers which provide day care. That would be another way to give the care-giver an opportunity for time off. Some centers provide what is known as respite care. They care for the victim for short periods, possibly two weeks, while the family takes a vacation.

6. A person who cares for a loved one with Alzheimer's should join a support group. These groups provide not only information about available resources, but also emotional support.

7. Ultimately your loved one will probably go to a full-time care center. It would be wise to study the alternatives ahead of time. Some centers that specialize in Alzheimer's disease may be a little less expensive than nursing homes, because Alzheimer's victims may not require the intense medical care needed by many nursing home patients.

8. If you should become the care-giver for an Alzheimer's victim, forgive yourself when you lose patience. You are doing a superhuman job, and you are only human.

In coping with a helpless loved one, we need friends, family, and the people in a support group. With God's help and with theirs, we will find that we have more inner strength and patience than we thought possible. We may find that we have drawn closer to our family and friends.

There is a striking passage in the Old Testament (Exodus 17:8-13), where the Hebrews are engaged in battle. As long as Moses keeps his hands raised, the battle goes well for the Hebrews. When his arms fall from weakness, the tide turns. So his friends come to his side and hold his arms up!

Inevitably people ask, "Why me?" There are no good answers to that question, but some people who have been in such predicaments have asked another question, "Why not me?" They have thought of the good things they experienced in their lives — a good marriage, children, secure employment. Some of our friends missed those things.

If you are angry with God, tell Him so. The Lord let David be angry with Him. If you don't think you can manage, tell Him that.

When you have opened your heart to God, you may not come away with pat, simple answers. But you will sense that underneath are the everlasting arms, that nothing can separate you from the love of God in Christ Jesus.

In our darkest hours we can put our hand into God's hand, confident that one day He will bring us into the light.

46.
"WHEN I WAS RAISING MY CHILDREN, I WAS CAREFUL ABOUT WHAT TV SHOWS AND MOVIES WE LOOKED AT AND WHAT BOOKS AND MAGAZINES WE READ. NOW THAT THEY'RE GONE, IT DOESN'T SEEM TO MAKE AS MUCH DIFFERENCE."

It does make a difference!

Isn't the feeding of our own minds important?

What does a violent film do to us? For some, it causes emotions of fear that may result in nightmares and bad dreams. These films may also desensitize us to the value of human life.

Is it possible that sexually explicit films may prompt us

to create and enjoy scenes of illegitimate sex in our minds? Jesus said this kind of thinking was as sinful as the immoral act.

Psychologists say that many thoughts seep down into the subconscious mind and trouble us long after they are forgotten on the conscious level.

As we indiscriminately view anti-Christian media, we may move slowly to adopt the world view of the media producers, many of whom have no place in their thinking for God and the Judeo-Christian moral teachings.

The Bible challenges us to keep our minds centered on what is true, honest, pure, lovely, and of good report. Paul wrote those words in Philippians 4:8 so that we would have good things to discuss with others. He also knew that what we think about all day has an effect on our souls.

When we decide to eliminate media garbage, we are not left in a vacuum. A smorgasbord of good things is available to enlighten and enrich our lives.

Some plays and movies are worth seeing. Check out the ratings and reviews and choose the best. Some of the best films of the past are on video. Choose some funny ones. Laughter is good for the soul.

Those who have cable TV find that the Discovery, Arts and Entertainment, Learning, and Travel channels offer fascinating programs.

Watch the book reviews and choose choice books that will inform and inspire you. One program on a C-Span channel called "Booknotes" allows authors to talk for an hour about serious books they have written.

How long has it been since you visited an art gallery, listened to a concert by the local symphony orchestra, or browsed through a museum?

How about looking at the biographies on the shelves of your local library? Make a list of those you might like to read in the next couple of years. Have you heard your pastor quote words from Francis of Assisi, or Martin Luther, or William Booth, founder of the Salvation Army? You might enjoy reading a biography of one of these men.

When we reject the media trash, we can substitute so much that will enrich our lives.

47.
"I HAVE AN OPPORTUNITY TO JOIN A GROUP OF SENIOR CITIZENS ON A TRIP TO A CASINO. IT'S A BARGAIN — TEN DOLLARS FOR BUS FARE, A BIG MEAL AND A PACKAGE OF QUARTERS TO PLAY THE MACHINES."

The initial sack of quarters may be free, but you are virtually sure to lose money if you engage in commercial gambling over a period of time. Unlike a poker game played in one's home, or an office pool where all the money stays in house, commercial gambling establishments program their machines and games to take a big slice of the money for overhead and profit. Even if one were lucky at the outset, continuous playing at a machine or gambling table would ultimately produce losses.

In the case of state lotteries, there are the costs for the gambling bureaucracy, the money taken to fund state projects, the commissions paid to retailers for selling the tickets, advertising and other expenses.

Some may respond, "I know all of this, but it's fun. I like to take risks. I like excitement."

Then you might want to consider the dangers of addiction to gambling, and the devastation that it has brought to thousands of families. Here are snatches of conversation that came over a compulsive gambling hotline phone.

"I lost my entire paycheck today playing pull tabs."

"The only thing my wife cares about is gambling, not her family, her job or anything else."

"I lost my semester's tuition at the casino."

"I wrote bad checks last night to cover $3,000 in losses at the casino."

"My husband is a recovering alcoholic, and now he's starting to act the same way with his gambling that he did when he was drinking."

"Both of my parents are retired and spend all of their time gambling. I don't know what to do."

Clearly, gambling is a problem for many people and a crippling addiction for some. In a study made by the Minnesota Department of Human Services, these figures were released: Seven percent of Minnesota adults and six percent of adolescents were identified as problem gamblers. The same law which established the Minnesota State Lottery also authorized the development of a program for the treatment of compulsive gamblers.

Do you want to risk that kind of addiction? Do you want to encourage others to take such a risk? As one man reflected on addictions, he said, "If I had a dog that bit one out of every nine persons, or even one out of fourteen, I would get rid of that dog."

Jesus said, "I am come that they might have life, and that they might have it more abundantly" (John 10:10 KJV). Is the excitement and risk involved in gambling the abundant life He was talking about?

If you want to experience excitement, if you would like to take some risks, here are some possible alternatives:

Volunteer as a camp counselor for some underprivileged kids. You may have some pranks played on you. You will work longer and harder than you did the last week you worked at your job. You may also make a difference in the life of someone who needs a role model.

Learn a skill that will enable you to do something new. You'll be excited as you try to keep up with younger people and pleased when you succeed.

Study some overseas area where missionary and relief work is carried on. Raise some money to help the people there.

Offer to mentor a young person in your community.

Consider volunteering for several months of service to help needy people, here or abroad.

God has something better for our lives than the non-productive and possibly self-destructive waste of time called *gambling*.

48.
"WHEN YOU THINK OF ALL THE TIME PEOPLE PUT INTO FITNESS CLUBS, MALL WALKING, ETC., DON'T PAUL'S WORDS, 'BODILY EXERCISE PROFITETH LITTLE,' APPLY?"

A more accurate rendering of 1 Timothy 4:8 is found in the New International Version, "For physical training is of some value, but godliness has value for all things, holding promise for both the present life and the life to come." This is a verse that sets priorities.

Paul's use of athletic metaphors indicates that he probably had an interest in sports and the physical training involved in preparing for them. But his priority is on training for godliness. That prepares us for life now and for eternity.

It could be argued that if Paul had lived in our time, he would have had more to say about physical exercise when he spoke of the body being the temple of the Holy Spirit (1 Corinthians 6:19). People in the ancient world used their bodies for tasks that we accomplish by pushing a button. Paul walked to the towns he visited. In fact, he walked across the Roman Empire.

We sit at computers and let our fingers do the walking. Modern technology seems bent on engineering physical exercise out of our lives, and in so doing opens us to the risk of life-shortening diseases.

A period of exercise several times a week in a fitness center is ideal. If we can't do that, we can block out a period of time to walk on the streets or in a mall. For people with conditions like arthritis, swimming is a good activity.

Beyond this, we can make it a point to use our bodies more. Walk to the mail box to mail a letter. Climb two flights of stairs rather than taking an elevator. If an errand is less than a mile, walk. Housework, gardening, shuffleboard — anything that causes us to move is beneficial. You will get big returns for a little bit of effort.

New research is discovering that we may not have to exercise 30-45 minutes. Three ten-minute periods during the day will help.

The payoff?

You will feel better and maybe look better.

If you combine exercise with a sensible diet, you will keep your weight under control.

You will feel more relaxed.

You may be easier to get along with.

Getting control of our bodies is a spiritual victory.

But we should emphasize the main teaching of the verse: Training in godliness is the priority. Taking steps that will make us more like Jesus is important for time and eternity.

That includes a time for personal and family devotions, attending worship in your local church, an occasional day set apart for reflection, and perhaps becoming a part of a small group where we pray and study the Bible with others.

Spiritual fitness means giving attention to situations in our lives that need changing, maybe being less irritable with our spouse, or not talking about the shortcomings of a friend except in the context of finding a way to help. Let us make one of these a prayer concern and chart our progress.

Spiritual fitness enables us to battle Satan. We learn what it means to be a prayer warrior, to use the Word of God, and to keep ourselves pure and unspotted from the world.

We will never experience the thundering roars that crowds give to football players receiving a touchdown pass. But as Hebrews 12:1 tells us, "....we are surrounded by such a great cloud of witnesses." Perhaps the angels in heaven are some of these witnesses. When we win spiritual victories, they may be shouting to celebrate our success.

49.
"I CAN'T SEEM TO REMEMBER NAMES AND ADDRESSES ANYMORE, I FORGET WHERE I PUT THINGS. I WONDER IF I'M LOSING MY MIND."

Most aging people face the problem of short-term memory loss.

A man can't remember what his wife told him to pick up at the store.

You go upstairs and forget why you are there.

There are long, intense searches for misplaced items and, like the woman who lost the coin in Jesus' parable, much rejoicing when the objects are found.

Even more distressing is that we remember times when we could process a great deal of material and recall it immediately. A retired school teacher remembers how she knew the names of every child in her class the second day of school. A business man used to carry around in his head the names, addresses, and many details about every one of his customers.

Short-term memory loss is a fact of life, but it doesn't mean that we are losing our minds.

We can do things to compensate. These strategies have helped some people:

Write things down that you want to remember. Put notes

to yourself on the refrigerator door or on the mirror in the bathroom.

Make copies of important papers and put them in two different places.

If you want to remember something you've read or your reaction to it, speak it into a tape recorder.

Mention something that you want to remember to a family member or friend. If it's an appointment to be kept, ask a friend to call you the day before to remind you.

You can develop other ways to cope. But the most important word to people experiencing short-term memory loss is to RELAX. Laugh at yourself.

Okay, you can't remember things the way you used to, but you are not going to worry about it. Chances are that lost items will surface and some day you will remember the forgotten information. Even if that doesn't happen, it's not the end of the world.

Instead, let us rejoice that there has been no loss of other mental faculties.

Most older people, including those experiencing short-term memory loss, have reasoning powers as strong or stronger than when they were young. We can reason, evaluate, figure things out.

Our experiences over many years provide a perspective that enables us to make wiser decisions than when we were young.

Older people are able to recall events early in life, and reflecting on these gives wisdom and satisfaction.

Let us stretch our minds, let us give ourselves challenges. Read an article on some issue that interests you in a magazine prepared for intellectuals. Join a grandchild in playing a computer game that demands reasoning power.

And yes, you can still memorize some things. Why not determine that you will memorize a dozen key Bible verses that will enrich your life? Start with a short one like, "The things which are impossible with men are possible with God" (Luke 18:27 KJV), or, "If God be for us, who can be against us?" (Romans 8:31 KJV). Then take on some longer ones such as, "They that wait upon the Lord shall renew their strength; they shall mount up with wings as eagles; they shall run, and not be weary; and they shall walk and not faint" (Isaiah 40:31 KJV). When you've memorized the 12 verses, treat yourself and a friend to a meal in a nice restaurant.

You can do it! We can still learn! We can acquire new information and learn new skills. It may take longer, but we can do it. And learning new things makes us sharper, more useful persons.

There are trade-offs as we age. We lose some things, we gain others. Let us rejoice in what we gain.

As Paul said in 1 Thessalonians 5:18, "...Give thanks in all circumstances."

50.
"EVERYDAY WE HEAR REPORTS OF MUGGINGS AND VIOLENT CRIME. I'M AFRAID TO GO OUT OF THE HOUSE."

The newscasts in many cities manage to report a violent crime almost every day. With good reason, that alarms us.

But we should put this in perspective. The nature of the news business is to report the unusual, the dramatic, the violent. The media must report an aircraft accident. They don't report the 99.99+% safe flights. The violent crime that is reported on the evening news is an exception. Even in large cities, the majority of people have never been attacked or robbed.

A study from the U.S. Justice Department reported that people over 65 are six times less likely to be crime victims than are younger people and eight times less likely to be victims of violent crime. The only exceptions were purse snatching and pickpocketing.

The same report indicated that the chances of older people being victims of criminal acts actually declined during the period 1973-1990.

This is not to say that seniors are not at risk. Some criminals do take advantage of the weaknesses of older people. Precautions should be taken and it would be a good idea for everyone to make a list of things she should do to lower the risk of a criminal attack. Such a list may include these precautions:

1. When walking for exercise, walk with a partner. Or, go to a mall where there are lots of people.

2. Think about purchasing a security system for your home and advertise it prominently so that burglars will pass you by.

3. When possible, plan activities during the daylight rather than at night.

4. When going out at night, try to go with someone else or perhaps arrange for transportation by taxi.

5. Do not invite any stranger into your home.

6. Trust your instincts. If you feel uncomfortable getting on an elevator with another person, don't get on.

7. Scan parking lots before approaching your car. If there are not many people around, don't be afraid to ask a door man or security guard for an escort.

Each person should make her special list.

But we should avoid a serious mistake. We can let ourselves be paralyzed by fear and retreat into a cocoon. God has given us a mission to accomplish. There are projects to complete, places to go, people to see, meetings to attend, classes to enjoy.

Long ago, the apostle Paul wrote to a young man, Timothy, who had a tendency to be fearful: "For God did not give us a spirit of timidity, but a spirit of power, of love and of self-discipline" (2 Timothy 1:7).

Remember that most people are not attacked. Take precautions, and then move ahead to do what God has called you to do.

When fear strikes, counter it with an affirmation of faith. Something like the words: "God has said, 'Never will I leave you; never will I forsake you.'"

And think of one other well-spoken affirmation: "When fear knocked at the door, faith answered. No one was there."

51.
"I DON'T LIKE TO INVITE PEOPLE TO MY HOME ANYMORE. I JUST CAN'T KEEP THE HOUSE THE WAY I USED TO."

One way to think about this is that your home is yours, and how you keep it is your business. If you are happy there, your guests should be too.

But questions like this suggest that it may be time to think about a new style of living. Do we have the right housing for this stage of our lives? Do we need a big house with all of the work involved in that? Would a town house or an apartment where the costs include maintenance make more sense?

If we decide to stay in a house which demands a lot of care, can we afford a cleaning service to do the heavy house cleaning and other chores? Perhaps the time has come to major on the things we can do best, and that may mean leaving the cleaning to someone else.

Jesus' parable about the man selling all that he had to buy the pearl of great price (Matthew 13:45,46) may have an application here. Is it time to focus on the good things God wants us to experience and unload the competing baggage?

We still want to entertain our friends. But, why fret about the energy and time required to prepare a meal for guests? The best solution may be to say, "Let's have lunch at a restaurant where we can spend an hour or two without being hustled out." If you have a coupon for a free meal with the purchase of another, it probably won't cost any more than serving a meal at home.

Most homes lived in for many years have too much furniture. Often, when real estate salespeople advise owners on getting their homes ready for sale, they say something like this "Take half of the furniture out of this room and put it in the garage. Less cluttered rooms make a house more attractive."

Could someone in your family use some of those pieces of furniture? If not, why not give them to the Salvation Army? You'll enjoy brighter, bigger rooms and someone else will get some good furniture.

And what about the files, books, letters you've been saving for years? Little by little, put an end to the clutter.

You thought you might read those magazines or books some day. You've been saying that for years. Are you really going to read them? Maybe they should go into a giant circular file.

How long should you keep files with cancelled checks and receipted bills? A few years, perhaps, but not ten or twenty.

And packs of letters? If they were letters your husband wrote during courtship days, tie a blue ribbon around them for reading on anniversaries. But, out with the rest of the letters.

Piles of paper can be depressing right now and some day may create a lot of work for a member of your family.

During his famous expedition, Admiral Richard Byrd discovered more than the South Pole. He said, "I am learning that man can live profoundly without masses of things."

The time has come to simplify.

52.
"A FRIEND OF MINE FAILED THE PHYSICAL FOR RENEWING HER DRIVER'S LICENSE. THAT WOULD DEVASTATE ME, I DON'T EVEN WANT TO THINK ABOUT IT."

It was reported that an older person told a visitor, "I'm having a hard time hearing and I don't see very well, but thank goodness I can still drive."

We laugh at that, but it points to a time that everyone of us must face. That is the day we must give up driving, preferably before failing a physical. However competent we feel now, the day will come when we should no longer be at the wheel of a car.

We read stories of elderly people who have accidents. One man whose car killed a child vowed that he would never drive again. If only he had made that decision earlier!

Yes, such accidents could happen to anyone. But slower reflexes and dimmer eyes increase the risk.

We should be thinking about how alert we are and how well we see. If we are having close calls, that should be a sign to us.

We may make the transition from driving to not driving in stages.

Many seniors decide that they will not drive at night. They sense they can't see as well at night and they're right.

Another limit would be to avoid driving during rush hours when heavy traffic makes accidents more likely.

Later, one might want to avoid the main highways altogether, just driving in well-known neighborhoods near home.

As the winding down takes place, we may experiment

with other forms of transportation. We will learn that we can have wheels even when we're not behind the wheel.

Some of us who haven't used trains or busses for years will find that kind of travel is not half bad, especially if we don't travel during rush hours.

We can use county-sponsored vans which provide a kind of taxi service for seniors and others in outlying areas.

We may arrange to go places and attend events with family members and friends. Tell them, "If you drive, I'll pay for the parking," or, "I'll buy the tickets."

When the cost of running a car is eliminated from our budget, we will be able to afford private taxis for some of our trips.

The good news is that when the time comes to stop driving, we will be able to continue most of our travel and have one less thing to worry about.

Is there any spiritual principle involved here? There is indeed! A well-known command of Jesus is "Love your neighbor as yourself" (Mark 12:31). Most of us don't enjoy driving with an incompetent driver and we don't want such drivers on the highways. When we know that we can't see well and react quickly, we shouldn't be driving a vehicle.

Let us decide that when that time comes, we will have the courage to say, "Now is the time to stop, I'm going to leave the driving to someone else."

53.
"I LIKE TO REVISIT THE PLACES WHERE I WAS RAISED. IS THAT A SIGN OF OLD AGE, OR WANTING TO LIVE IN THE PAST?"

It's healthy to revisit places that have meant a lot to us during our early years. Our reflections on those times and places can enrich our lives today and tomorrow.

In the Bible, David expressed a bit of nostalgia when he

asked, "Oh, that someone would get me a drink of water from the well near the gate of Bethlehem!" (2 Samuel 23:15).

I think that our grown children would like to know about their roots. They might even appreciate a booklet containing our written memoirs with some good photos.

Here are some important places and events in my life.

One is the school yard where I played "punch" ball. What important thing happened there? During a time when I wasn't being chosen to play on the teams, I still remember the words of one friend, "Will is a good player."

At high school, what teachers, what activities were important? What books did we read in English literature? It might be fun to read some of them again — books like George Eliot's *Silas Marner* or Nathaniel Hawthorne's *The Scarlet Letter.* Or, if we don't feel like reading the books, we could listen to them on tape. We didn't have enough experience during our teen years to really appreciate those books. A rereading now would not only bring back memories, but could also enrich our lives and give us new insights.

What was the first job that paid real money? What memories of the boss? I remember my paper route. Most of the customers paid promptly and many of them gave me a tip. But I still remember one oddball customer on that route. I had to return many times to collect the twenty-five cents owed me. Whoever had the money in that household was always in the bathtub.

What about the possibility of attending the church where we were raised? What memories do we have of the day of our baptism or confirmation? Who were the young people in the church during those times? Where are they now? What pastor meant the most to us? What made him effective?

What are our memories of Thanksgiving and Christmas seasons?

What were some other important firsts in our lives?

The first time I was able to get enough money together to see a major league baseball game was an important day in my life. It was a double header between the Brooklyn Dodgers and Cincinnati Reds.

If we decided to put together a booklet with some of these memories for our families, we should make the writing as attractive as possible. We might even ask someone to work with us in writing this out. Eliminate boring details, emphasize anecdotes — little stories that make a point. Try to include some humor. We should choose the best pictures we can find to illustrate the booklet.

If we gave a booklet like this to our family members, it would not be forgotten. In fact, it might be passed on to grandchildren and great grandchildren.

No, relishing the memories of past days isn't a sign of old age. It doesn't mean that we are living in the past. In reviewing past events, we may come to see our lives today in a new light. We may gain perspective that will help us plan happy adventures for the future.

The Greek poet, Sophocles, wrote: "One must wait until evening to see how lovely the day has been."

Your journey into bygone days may give you the same feeling. You may feel like saying, "Thank you Lord, the day has been a lovely one indeed."

PART III

Developing Positive
Personal Relationships

54.
"I FEEL THAT OUR MARRIAGE RELATIONSHIP IS GOING TO CHANGE AFTER WE RETIRE."

Yes, it will. The nature of the change was well described by the wry comments of two women.

"In retirement, I have half as much income and twice as much husband."

"I married him for better or for worse, but not for lunch."

Every couple will have a unique solution to the changes in the marriage relationship. But, here are some guidelines.

1. It's probably not possible, nor desirable, to do every thing together. Retirement doesn't change the fact that a husband and wife have different gifts and interests. Those differences mean that a man or a woman will do some things alone.

One couple, both of whom were employed full time, retired the same year. Not long after retirement the wife had an opportunity to become a receptionist in a restaurant in town. Though she wanted the job, her husband protested. They didn't need the money and she would be away most evenings. But she liked meeting new people and she required something to give shape to her day. After discussion, she took the job and her husband now accepts her work.

Let a wife encourage her husband to do his thing in some room in the house without always cleaning it up and complaining about the mess he makes. Encourage him to go with friends on a fishing trip or to a ball game.

In fact, encourage your spouse to do what makes him/her happy. Garage sales tire me out. I can't imagine anything more boring than to peer at piles of junk. But garage sales energize my wife. She gets a gleam in her eye when she learns about a new one. She comes home with great bargains for us, our children, and our grandchildren. I tell her where there are new sales. Periodically, I bring packets of fifty one-dollar bills from the bank to facilitate her purchases.

2. However, retirement brings opportunities to do more things together. It will be a time to fulfill dreams expressed through the years, "If we ever have time, we'd like to ..."

Some couples look forward to traveling. If those trips are carefully planned, they can provide happy times. If you can't afford long trips, there are dozens of outings you can do within fifty miles of your home.

One couple took a slow train ride through beautiful country near Stillwater, Minnesota. They were served an elegant meal on an old-fashioned train. That and dozens of other such excursions could provide enriching days for retired couples.

Do some of these things while you are still able!

3. The retirement years may provide special times to serve the Lord.

Every local church could enrich its ministry. If you have more time, you could strengthen your church's outreach.

Here are some opportunities you might consider:

Are there people in your community who can't read or who have poor reading skills? Consider starting a program to teach them.

Do the chaplains in local nursing homes, hospitals, prisons, or half-way houses need help?

Are you into crafts that others might like to learn? You could help a youngster or a senior learn to do something useful with their hands.

What about asking the pastor of your church for the names of three shut-ins whom you could make your special responsibility?

Have you thought of volunteering for six months service on one of your church's mission fields?

In such activities a husband or wife could work together or they could work individually. Sometimes different skills can be used in the same setting. During a year's service overseas, one husband worked as an accountant while his wife performed a variety of useful chores for the mission.

Even when you're not working together, a husband and wife can cheer each other on. One couple I know works with prisoners. Each has a separate assignment, but they are deeply interested in how the Lord is working in the other's service. They rejoice together when one of them experiences a victory.

Establish a goal to help your partner become all that God intended him/her to be. If you do that, your retirement years will be beautiful ones indeed.

55.
"I UNDERSTAND WHY OLDER COUPLES DIVORCE. I STILL WANT TO BE SEXUALLY ACTIVE, BUT MY SPOUSE NO LONGER SEEMS INTERESTED IN SEX."

A faulty sexual relationship is usually related to the total way a man and woman feel about each other.

There's almost nothing a woman won't do for a man

who makes her feel good about herself. And the same thing can be said about a man.

Men are captivated by women who make them feel more capable, more intelligent, sexier. A man wants to know why he makes a difference to a woman. He wants to hear it again and again.

If a man puts a new roof on the house, his wife should tell him how lucky she is to have a man who can do things that save so much money.

If he is active in the church, let her tell him how happy she is to have a man who loves God's work.

If he has taught the children to do practical things, tell him how fortunate they have been to have a father like him.

It won't hurt to repeat statements like this and then add new affirmations. A husband will do almost anything to live up to the compliments of his wife.

Women talk easily, a lot of men do not. But there are times when a man wants to be listened to. If his wife is there to listen, trying to understand his feelings instead of giving advice, she will be appreciated.

Husbands also need to demonstrate to their wives that they are worth a lot to them, that they could not live without them.

Think about turning differences into compliments.

If a wife is practical and her husband is not, let him tell her how wonderful it is to have a woman who keeps their financial condition stable.

To put excitement into the marriage write a romantic letter, spend a night with her in a hotel, plan a surprise trip.

Let him talk often about how important she is to him.

That women need to hear how valuable they are was illustrated in a story from Polynesia. A man fell in love with a young girl who was disliked by her family. In this society, a man who wanted to marry a woman paid her family a brideprice, usually in cows. This young woman's family would have been glad to get rid of their daughter for one cow. But her suitor shocked the village by offering eight cows. When asked why he gave so many, he said, "I want everybody to know that my new wife is worth a lot." Later, when friends came to visit, they were amazed to see that this young woman had changed from an ugly, dejected girl to an attractive, happy young woman.

If there is communication, if there are a stream of loving, affirming comments, if each spouse tries to build up the other's self-esteem , the sexual part of marriage will improve.

In every marriage there will be arguments. If they are handled the right way, even these can lead to passionate love encounters. Discuss the problem in a quiet setting. Concentrate on solving the problem, not winning an argument.

Use "I feel" statements instead of general accusations. Rather than, "You are so thoughtless," it would be better to say, "I was upset when you didn't call me."

If you can say, "That was my fault, please forgive me," you will be on the way to restoring the relationship.

A Christian couple has one more important resource. They can talk together with God. A New York City pastor who had married hundreds of couples said that he never heard of the divorce of a couple who followed through on a promise to pray together.

Happy marriages — it's a matter of talking with each other and with God.

56.
"I WISH THAT MY SPOUSE AND I COULD DIE THE SAME DAY. I CAN'T IMAGINE OUR LIVING APART."

Unless you are killed in an air crash, you probably won't

die the same day. One spouse is likely to live several years after the other goes. The most loving thing you can do is to prepare now for that day when one of you will be without the other.

You may start by making sure that both of you know what the other does to manage the home. One time when my wife was away, I flooded the kitchen with soapy water when I tried to use the dishwasher. That taught me that it is better to learn under supervision. If a wife does most of the housework, let the husband learn how she operates the washer and dryer. Let him try the blender and the microwave. Let him go shopping with her and learn how she saves money.

One member of the marriage team may manage the finances. Let the other member do it for two months, asking questions when needed. Who makes out the income tax forms? Let the other do it under supervision. If a tax preparer is employed, help the other member assemble the necessary papers.

When a spouse dies, how will the survivor live for another ten years? A couple should take pencil and paper and determine exactly how much the other will have to live on. If the husband dies, how much, if any, of his pension will continue for his wife? How much will the survivor receive from Social Security? How long will income from investments last? If most of the income is fixed, how far will that go five years down the road with even a modest increase in inflation? Could one person manage the costs of living in the same house? If it seems advisable to go into a retirement community, would there be money for that?

When it seems that the survivor will be short of money, one option for taking care of the lack might be additional life insurance. Another might be to arrange for what is called a reverse mortgage that would provide income from the equity accumulated in a home. A financial advisor or a lawyer should be brought into these discussions.

Some Christians may pass off this advice with a comment such as, "The Lord has always taken care of us, He will take care of the one who survives." Such words might be backed up with a verse such as, "Therefore do not worry about tomorrow..." (Matthew 6:34).

That verse carries a great truth — God does provide for His children. It is especially true in situations where we have little control over events like the weather and illness. We know that whatever happens, we are never outside of the love of our heavenly Father.

It is also true that few people in our country starve to death. In case of financial emergency, children or relatives may help. The government has safety nets for the impoverished. But, why expect our children to support us, or even the taxpayers, when we can plan ahead for ourselves?

It is interesting to note that Jesus Himself made plans for future events. He sent two disciples ahead to find a donkey for His entry into Jerusalem (Matthew 21:2), and He sent ahead to reserve a room for the Last Supper (Matthew 26:18). Paul made plans for the collection of an offering that was to be used to help famine victims in Jerusalem (1 Corinthians 16:1-4).

The overall teaching of Scripture is: If we can plan, let us ask God to help us do that. If we cannot plan ahead, trust the Lord to provide.

The uncertainty of life challenges us to make the best of the years that remain. Have we thought about visiting a sister who lives in another state? Have we talked about giving a week of service to build a Habitat for Humanity home? Have we played with the idea of spending several months as volunteers in an overseas mission field? Let's do one project next year and another one the following year. A couple might even think together of worthwhile activities for the survivor.

When the time of parting comes, the spouse who remains will be able to say, "We planned well. We had good times during our retirement years, and we decided that the one who lived on should have more."

57.

"I DON'T WANT TO BE A BURDEN TO MY CHILDREN DURING MY LAST YEARS."

Most of us feel this way. We don't want to depend on our children for care and we don't want them burdened with extra financial responsibilities. Many older people know that they would not want to live with their children.

How different it was several decades ago!

My grandfather's last employment ended at age 65 in 1930. He had no pension. There was no social security. He had no savings. For eighteen years, until his death in 1949, he depended entirely upon my single aunts. They provided his support including pocket money, carfare and medical expenses. In the early years of his retirement he would have worked, if there had been work to do. But during those depression years, millions of younger people were unemployed.

My aunts were glad they could support their parents. They believed that was their mission in life.

Fortunately, adult children don't have the responsibilities that existed two generations ago. Most adults have Social Security and many have pensions which make it possible to live without depending on our children. Government safety nets such as Medicare and Medicaid assure us that we will be cared for when we are ill.

Perhaps your adult children will have to arrange for your final care. That is life. When they are old, their children will help them.

If we want to lighten the burden that remains, here are

some things to think about.

Do you have a will, drawn by a lawyer, where you have clearly provided for the disposition of your estate, including the physical objects in your home? Have you named the person who should be executor of your estate?

Have you made a living will which authorizes doctors to discontinue heroic measures to keep you alive? You can inform your children about this now so they will not have to make this decision.

Have you considered entering a retirement community with nursing home facilities? That would reduce your adult children's responsibilities.

Is there money set aside for your funeral and burial? If you wish, you may decide ahead of time to make that less expensive than it would normally be.

Have you informed your family about where your important papers are located? Does a member of your family have a key to your safe deposit box?

Have you designated someone who will have power of attorney in the event that you become disabled?

Some elderly people who have sufficient financial resources become an emotional burden to their adult children. A friend told me that her father insisted that she call him several times a day. He also called her frequently. He often felt sick when they were about to leave for a weekend vacation. We should determine now that we will not impose that kind of emotional burden on our adult children.

The best thing we can say to older people who are concerned about being a burden is that God loves us and has promised to be faithful to the end. Let us trust in these words written by Isaiah, "When you pass through the waters, I will be with you; and when you pass through the rivers, they will not sweep over you..." (Isaiah 43:2a).

58.

"MY CHILDREN DON'T CALL ME FOR WEEKS AT A TIME. I WONDER, ARE THEY JUST THOUGHTLESS? HAVE I OFFENDED THEM?"

"They only call when they want money."

"They forget all the sacrifices I made for them."

"They're so busy, they have no time for me."

While we express our hurt feelings, let us turn our minds in another direction.

That our adult children don't need us any more is, in a way, a tribute to the fact that we raised them to be self-sufficient, independent adults.

Let us realize also that we should not expect a return for the sacrifices we made to raise them. Think of it this way — our sons and daughters are paying us back by sacrificing to raise their own children.

It's nice to receive gratitude, but we still have the satisfaction of knowing we did our best for our children.

What might be the reasons for the absence of telephone calls?

Our adult children may be very busy. If we are retired, the chances are that they are a lot busier than we are.

They might not enjoy the tone of our conversations. Is our talk negative, complaining? We think that our family should be concerned about our health and maybe they should, but people don't really enjoy listening to a recital of woes.

They may think that we preach too much. Even when they know the sermons are true, most young adults don't enjoy hearing them from their parents.

Indeed, there may be some unresolved issue that has caused their coldness.

If our children are not calling us, let us take the initiative and call them. Choose a time when they may not be busy. Make the calls short, five to ten minutes. Decide ahead of time about how to make the conversation upbeat. Inquire about their lives and their children's. Share some good news. Close the conversation with the words, "I love you."

And if there is a barrier, then it's doubly important that we take the first step. In Mark 11:26 we read, "And when you stand praying, if you hold anything against anyone, forgive him, so that your Father in heaven may forgive you your sins."

That doesn't mean that we are wrong. But we want to rebuild our relationship. We still love our children.

In the Parable of the Prodigal Son, the father had no way to make a long distance call, but when he saw his son a long way off, he ran to meet him.

Let us be ready for reconciliation.

Our sad feelings may be the result of loneliness. Our lives have been tied up with our children's and now we must reach out in other directions. It's time to find new friends, new avenues of service, new opportunities to learn.

We still love our adult children, we will never exclude them from our lives. But our happiness no longer depends on them.

59.
"I WAS CRUSHED WHEN TWO OF MY CHILDREN FORGOT ME ON MOTHER'S DAY."

An empty mail box on Saturday, and a silent telephone on Mother's Day Sunday are enough to make a mother cry.

Go ahead and cry. Then think about doing one of these things:

It may help to share your hurt with a friend.

Some people have written a letter to the person who has hurt them and then torn it up.

I have a friend who wrote a poem to express her sorrow at being forgotten on Mother's Day.

Cry, in one way or another, and then wait for the sun to come out. It will shine again for you if you think about these things.

Whether they acknowledge it or not, the love and effort you put into raising your children will never be lost. Your children are what they are today in great measure because of their parents. Nothing can change that.

The Christian training you gave your children is influencing their lives. Whether your adult children are practicing Christians or not, they will never escape the influence of their parents' Christian lives.

If your children are caring well for their own children, they are, in a sense, paying you back. You modeled for them what a parent should be. Consider yourself honored if they reflect your attitudes in raising their own children.

The sun will also come out for you if you pray the right way about your thoughtless children. In your prayers, remember first all of the people who have been gracious to you. That will condition your mind with love. Then pray for the children who have forgotten you. Thank God for them, for what they have accomplished, for the good things they are doing in the world. Then pray for their health and prosperity. Pray that God's will be done in their lives. If this is hard to do, repeat these prayers often. Little by little the hurt will disappear.

Follow up your prayers with the normal communications you would have with your children. In your letters and phone calls, let them know that you love them.

God's sunlight will shine on you if you focus on the good things He has for you in the future. We must get on with our lives. Whether our children remember us or not, the time when our lives and theirs were closely intertwined is past. Our happiness no longer depends upon them. We still have a journey to travel which may mean embarking on a new career, learning a new skill, forming relationships with new associates and friends, accepting new opportunities to serve.

Prepare an agenda of satisfying, useful activities for each day. Among these will be occasional contacts with your adult children. Carry them out with enthusiasm and joy. But you have more in your life now.

Don't let resentments spoil the joys God has planned for you.

60.
"MY DAUGHTER IS GETTING A DIVORCE. I THINK I FEEL WORSE THAN SHE DOES—I KEEP ASKING MYSELF WHAT WENT WRONG."

Many older people have assumed that divorce couldn't happen in their families. But they are seeing that happen. Even well-known preachers have been saddened by the divorce of one or more of their children.

This is not a time to blame yourself or anyone else. If you trained your children in the Christian faith and taught them Christian values, you did your best. If you made mistakes—and all of us have made them—you can claim God's forgiveness. And you should forgive yourself.

Remember that your adult child is probably grieving much more than you are. In times like this we must try to feel something of the suffering our loved one is going through.

It's not the time for an attitude that communicates the idea, "How could you do this to us?"

Realize that your child is entering a grieving process and that you can be there to help her through it. A divorce requires a time of grief similar to that experienced when someone dies. Encourage your child to weep, to express her anger, even to complain to God.

God permits His children to be angry. David shows his anger in the Psalms. In Psalm 22:1 he cries out: "My God, my God, why have you forsaken me? Why are you so far from saving me, so far from the words of my groaning?"

But, as he works his way through the psalm, David says finally in verse 24: "For he (God) has not despised or disdained the suffering of the afflicted one; he has not hidden his face from him but has listened to his cry for help."

At an appropriate moment you can share some of God's truths for this situation. These might include:

Your daughter may not feel like forgiving her spouse, but God can help her, if she sets her mind in that direction.

Whatever happens, God is capable of moving her to new experiences, new friends, new accomplishments.

A wise parent may point a daughter or son to special help such as a support group for recently divorced persons or mediation services to help with issues such as custody and visitation.

Let your child know that you are going to stand beside her in the days ahead. She may need a temporary home, help in caring for her children, or financial aid to train for a new job. You will do what you can.

You can be the messenger of hope to your child. No matter how desperate she feels now, she can come to a deeper understanding of herself. She may experience a new vision of life's possibilities and a new sense of God's power in the midst of suffering.

You can communicate the assurance that when we have passed through the night of grief, there will be a morning of sunlight and new hope.

Divorce is ugly. It leaves scars. But God has not abandoned the divorced person. God can make her a more loving, more compassionate person.

61.
"I DON'T WANT MY CHILDREN FIGHTING OVER MY MONEY WHEN I AM GONE."

Our decisions about the disposal of our estate will have an effect on one or perhaps two generations ahead. It won't be just the money we leave, but also our way of thinking about its distribution.

A biblical guide for deciding this question comes from Micah 6:8: "He has showed you, O man, what is good. And what does the Lord require of you? To act justly and to love mercy and to walk humbly with your God."

The prophet makes three points that apply to making wills.

We should act justly. Our families have expectations and needs. Some have received more from us than others. We feel that we want to treat each of our children fairly, and a will may even out the distributions we have already made.

But there is also mercy. Some of our family members have greater needs than others. There is Christian work that we may want to help support after we have gone.

As we think about making a will, we must walk humbly before God. It is an act that demands God's wisdom. A husband and wife need the Lord's guidance to pass on what He has graciously enabled them to accumulate.

Everyone should consider these two points in making a will:

1. After we have asked God's help in making our decisions, we need a lawyer who can draw a will that cannot be misunderstood and which cannot be challenged. A lawyer may also help us understand ways of arranging our estate that may not have occurred to us.

2. We are not obligated to inform our families, but telling them about our decisions may reduce the possibility for

121

misunderstandings.

Some questions that have spiritual dimensions may include the following:

Suppose we want to leave something to our church or to a Christian organization. This is our privilege. It will make it easier if we explain to our children and others why this project is important to us. We will tell them that we love them and that we are leaving them a fair share of what we have.

Some of our children are better off than others. Should we leave each one the same amount? The situation of a single daughter with a good income is quite different from that of a son with five children. One way to address such a situation might be to leave each child the same amount, but to put a sum of money in trust for the education of each grandchild.

What about a child who has rejected us and our values? We should carefully consider whether we want to use our will to punish him. We have always tried to give all of our love to each child. And Christian love is free — it doesn't demand a return from the person who receives it. What do we want to say about our love for our children when we pass on?

And what about sharing some of our resources with our children while we are still alive? We could have the joy of seeing some of our estate used for projects that could bring us great satisfaction. If we are in our fifties and our children in their twenties or thirties, this may be the time when they need help. If we die in our eighties, by that time they may be well established in life.

Does one of our children need help to complete graduate school, or to put a down payment on a house, or to begin a business? Now may be the time to make our money count.

The distribution of our earthly goods will say a lot about

who we are and what we stand for.

Let us consider how to make that statement well.

62.
"I DON'T FEEL THAT I CAN CARE FOR MY GRANDCHILDREN WHILE MY DAUGHTER WORKS, YET I FEEL GUILTY WHEN I REFUSE HER."

Many grandparents are caring for grandchildren today. Sometimes they become the virtual parents.

Some are happy about this. They have experience, they like parenting, and they still have the energy to cope with young children. Some feel that they are giving their grandchildren a Christian training they might not otherwise receive.

Others care for their grandchildren reluctantly. They feel obligated to help their children. These grandparents complain:

"It's hard for me to keep up with kids at my age."

"I was looking forward to time for travel and hobbies when I retired, but that's impossible now."

"I'd like to work outside the home myself, even if it's only part-time."

What is right?

There is no "right" answer as to whether we should say yes or no to a request to care for grandchildren. The path to a good decision involves taking the Christian teaching on vocation seriously. Whether we are twenty-five or sixty-five, each of us has a calling to perform some kind of service. Each of us has a unique set of spiritual gifts and natural talents to complete that calling. We need to understand our gifts. We also need to pray for God's leading about how to use them. The "right" answer will come when, through prayer and reflection, we determine what God is calling us to do.

If God's leading seems to be that we care for our grand-children, so be it. Let us rejoice that we have an opportunity to provide loving, Christian care for another generation of little ones. When we make that decision, it should be our decision. It will be based on our understanding of God's will for our lives.

If we make the opposite choice, we shouldn't feel guilty. We are in charge of our lives. We are accountable only to the Lord. Be ready when a statement like this is made or implied:

"You have plenty of time, you can do this or that."

A key to living in retirement or semi-retirement is to plan our lives. We don't sit around waiting for things to happen. Even if it's a daily time for rest or periods of travel, we have the right to decide those things. We should take the initiative in planning our schedules and insist that family members respect our decisions.

If we are purposeful and clear about managing our lives, our children will respect us.

If we say to our adult children, "I love the kids and I'll be willing to help out in emergencies, but I'm too busy to take on regular child care now," our children will find another way.

Never feel guilty about doing what God has called you to do!

63.

"I WISH THERE WAS SOMETHING I COULD DO TO RAISE THE SELF-ESTEEM OF MY GRANDCHILDREN. THEIR PARENTS ALWAYS SEEM TO BE PUTTING THEM DOWN."

It's easy to criticize our adult children, but we need to remember that they have the twenty-four hour responsibility for their youngsters. We enjoy them for a few hours and then go home. We may have been just as impatient when our children were small.

Still, it is true that some parents are not doing the right things to build their children's self-esteem.

A child's excited words, "Look Dad, I got two A's on my report card," should not receive the response, "Son, I won't be happy until you get that C up also." Or, a daughter who tells her mother, "Surprise, I've washed and dried the dishes," should not hear, "Did you mop the floor?"

They may need to improve, but kids need affirmation and praise for what they do accomplish.

Is there anything grandparents can do? If you have personal contact with your grandchildren, you can do a lot.

Grandparents can make it a point to look for things to praise. When the child shows a report card with some improvement, tell him, "You make grandmother so proud." When a job has been well done, tell your granddaughter, "You've been a big help to me today."

It's also important to say something positive when nothing good is happening. Be generous with hugs and words like, "I'm so glad you belong to me," or, "Each day I love you more."

Grandparents can listen to their grandchildren. For a person of any age, just knowing that another human being is listening and taking her seriously is a boost to her self-esteem. Be attentive, mirror back some of the things she says, ask questions, let her know you consider her words important.

Nothing helps a child's self-esteem more than excelling in school activities. Playing an instrument in the school band or being one of the respected basketball players in the gym lifts a young person's self-esteem. In some cases, it might be possible for grandparents to offer to send their grandchild to a basketball camp or to pay for music lessons.

Make dates with grandchildren. Take them to places like the circus, or a mall where some exciting things are happening. Let them buy a fun meal at a fast food restaurant. Those days will be remembered.

When possible, let us attend the events that are meaningful in the lives of our grandchildren — a daily vacation Bible school graduation, a school play, or an athletic contest. If a young person performs well in some activity, let us congratulate her. Perhaps we might write a note telling her how well she did. When I wrote such a note to my daughter in appreciation of her part in a school play, she taped the note to her bedroom door where it remained for months.

A child needs heroes. As the poet said, "Lives of great men all remind us, we can make our lives sublime." Why not pick out books that describe inspiring lives and give them to your grandchildren? Read them the stories if they are not yet able to read. Share stories of young people who have overcome obstacles, one of whom said, "With Christ in my life, I can do anything."

Let your grandkids know that they can be heroes too. You have confidence in them. When you see evidence of a gift God has given to a child, tell her about it. You might say something like, "A girl who can figure out things that fast might be an accountant some day." We tend to move toward goals that some significant person thinks we can achieve.

There is no greater challenge than helping another human being become all that God meant him to be. And there's no better place to begin than with our grandchildren.

64.
"WHAT ELSE CAN GRANDPARENTS DO TO HELP THEIR GRANDCHILDREN?"

We can enrich the lives of our grandchildren by helping

them appreciate their family heritage.

When I was a child, I visited my grandparents twice a year. I still remember some of my grandfather's stories. He told me about his work as a buyer in John Wanamaker's store in Philadelphia, and his fishing trips on the Croydon River outside the city. I learned about him going without lunch to buy my grandmother's engagement ring. He described his first home, a fine house with brownstone trimmings that he rented for $25.00 a month. Grandpa went to church all his life, but he remembered best the visits he made to help organize a men's Bible class.

When my son was about ten, I remember him saying, "Dad, tell me stories about what you did when you were a boy." I think that my grandchildren will be interested in knowing some of the highlights of their grandparents' early lives.

Let our grandchildren look through a photo album and ask why the pictures are all black and white. Let them laugh at the silly clothing people wore and the ancient cars they drove in the 40s and 50s. Talk about the pictures of happy events and the circumstances surrounding them.

Did members of your family serve in World War II, or in one of the more recent wars? Was there anyone in the family who served as an overseas missionary? Let's tell our grandchildren about these people. What were other achievements of sisters, brothers and cousins?

If you live in the town where you were raised, your grand children will enjoy seeing the schools you attended. What teachers do you remember? What subjects did you like best? What classics did you study in English classes? Were you on any teams? Do you remember any special games? How did you feel when you graduated?

Talk to your grandchildren about the churches you attended when you were young. How did you come to receive Christ as personal Savior? How did you feel on the day of your confirmation or baptism? What pastors made the greatest impression on you? What did the young people do to have fun in those days?

Share with your grandchildren the times when you felt that God was especially important in your life. These experiences will make an impression on them.

Families in Israel constantly reminded their children and grandchildren about how God had worked in their history. They repeated often the stories of the Exodus and the entry into the Promised Land. Their interest in genealogies showed the importance of preserving the heritage of the Jewish people.

Providing links to the past will give our grandchildren a sense of security. They are part of a family which makes us all proud.

65.
"MY MOTHER SOMETIMES SAYS , 'I WISH YOU LIVED NEARER. I DON'T HAVE ANYONE ELSE TO TURN TO.' THAT MAKES ME FEEL GUILTY."

People are living a lot longer. Older middle-aged persons and young seniors are concerned about elderly parents in their seventies, eighties and older.

Two verses of Scripture help put our responsibilities to our parents into perspective. Genesis 2:24 (KJV) tells us, "Therefore shall a man leave his father and his mother, and shall cleave unto his wife: and they shall be one flesh." The key words in this King James translation rhyme, "leave" and "cleave." They indicate that our responsibility to our spouse and children has priority over other relationships. If we must live a thousand miles away from our home town for career or other reasons, that is where we should be. It's nothing to feel guilty about.

But the Scriptures show us also that we have obligations to our parents and others in our family. "If anyone does not provide for his relatives, and especially for his immediate family, he has denied the faith and is worse than an unbeliever" (1 Timothy 5:8).

Happily, 20th century technology makes it possible to leave and still stay in touch with our parents and other relatives. Saturday phone calls are inexpensive — ten minutes for a little more than a dollar. Before dialing, think of upbeat news and some affirming words. If there are children or grandchildren around, let them talk with Grandma or Granddad.

On special days like Christmas, Easter, birthdays or anniversaries a family might arrange for a conference call that would include parents and all the children. That would remind elderly parents of times when the whole family was together in the living room.

And you can keep the mailman busy. Even if Mom and Dad don't reply, keep sending them short, newsy letters. Include new pictures of your children and grandchildren. Recall happy experiences of your childhood. Express appreciation for the positive influence of your parents on your life.

If you could afford a visit to Mom and Dad once a year, or if you could bring them to your home for a couple of weeks, that would be a time that all would anticipate. If you plan well, that visit could become a highlight of the year.

Showing concern like this can make parents feel as close to you as they would to an adult child who lived 10 miles away.

But Mom's words, "I wish you lived nearer. I don't have anyone else to turn to," keep coming back. She is talking about a time when her life will change or when an emergency comes. She is telling you that she is going to feel alone. That is something to think about.

During most of their senior years our parents don't need our intervention in their affairs. Many older people spend their entire lives in their own homes. They make their own financial decisions. More often than not, they understand their needs and are capable of taking appropriate action.

Adult children shouldn't try to fix something that doesn't need fixing.

But when life changes and crises occur, what then? What can we do from a distance of a thousand miles?

The answer is plenty.

We can check out the resources available to help elderly people as they become less able to care for themselves. In most communities there are many. They include home delivery of meals, transportation, cleaning and shopping services, home health care, tax aid, counseling by telephone and in person, and many more. Some agencies will even make a daily call to an elderly person to make sure that all is well.

You can find out about the services in your parents' community by calling the United Way or the county's department of social services.

Mom and Dad may need help in housing changes. Again, some preliminary work can be done long before the time comes. You can find out about apartments, sheltered care, retirement communities and nursing homes in their community. Which are in their financial range? When the time comes, you are ready with options.

You can prepare for a crisis by checking out the adequacy of parents' health insurance. In an emergency, who could be called to help until you get there? Do you have the phone numbers of the family doctor, the pastor, close neighbors and friends, and nearby family members?

You can do a lot from a distance. Your concern may prompt a parent to say, "I feel so close to Eleanor. She lives a thousand miles away, but I feel as though she is around the corner."

66.
"I DREAD TO THINK OF BEING WITH MY MOTHER WHEN SHE DIES. I WON'T KNOW WHAT TO SAY."

A dying loved one brings us face to face, not only with her mortality, but also our own — an idea not pleasant to deal with.

To relate well to a dying family member, we need to renew our faith in Christ and His promises of eternal life. A parable comparing birth and death may be helpful here and might even be shared with the person we are caring for.

A child in her mother's womb is warm and secure. If that baby knew that she would leave her mother's body and enter another world, she might say, "I want to stay here."

But when the day comes for her to be born she finds that she likes her new world. People hold her and feed her. She discovers that she is loved.

That will be the experience of a Christian man or woman who dies. As a member of the family of God, the believer moves into a world that is filled with light and love, a world from which he will not want to return.

If you have this Christian hope, you will be a blessing to your loved one in her last days.

Some of the specific questions that may come up include:
Should I call the pastor?
What if she wants to talk about her funeral?
If she wants me to pray, what should I say?
What if she asks whether she is truly a child of God?
Follow the lead of your loved one. When she brings up a question, deal with it. When she wants to talk, be ready to converse with her.

131

If your mother wants to speak with a pastor, call him. If she doesn't want to see him, that does not mean she lacks respect for him or the church. She may not feel like meeting with anyone.

If she wants to discuss her funeral, listen. She may want to have a hymn sung or played, some special passage of Scripture read, or perhaps even a statement read to the gathering.

Sometimes your mother may want to talk about past experiences. Share memories with her. This might be the time to bring out an album of photos and let her reminisce about happy days in the past.

If Mom is angry about someone in the family, about her own condition, perhaps even with God, let her say that. She may wonder if God is angry with her. If she brings up something that she feels guilty about, you can listen and assure her that God is ready to forgive. Remind her that Jesus died for her sins, and He promised that anyone who trusts Him becomes a member of God's family.

You might make a prayer like this, "Lord Jesus, thank you for Mom's life. We know that You love her, and that You sent your Son to die on the cross for us all. Right now, we ask for forgiveness and assurance of salvation for her." Then you could ask her to say, "Amen," or to squeeze your hand if she wants this to be her prayer.

When it seems appropriate to read the Bible, ask her if there is a passage she would like to hear. Some good passages are John 14:1-6, 1 Corinthians 15:51-58, Psalm 46 and Psalm 121.

The last illness is not always a period of steady decline. There are times when a loved one will seem stronger. Before the end, there may be a surge of energy.

Those who have spent time with the dying have identified several stages, including denial, anger, bargaining, depression, and acceptance. All of these may not occur and they may not take place in this order. When a loved one passes through one or more of these stages, listen and assure her of your love.

Your presence, your sharing may help Mom discover God in a new way. She may come to a new sense of the meaning of God's love. You may help her come to a clearer view of that better Kingdom ahead.

When one little boy asked his mother what it meant to die, she turned her back at first and wept. Then she returned to the bedside and said, "John, you remember the times when you fell asleep in the living room. Without waking you, Daddy carried you to your room. The next morning you woke up in a different place, with the sunlight of a new day lighting your room. That is death, John. We go to sleep in one room, and we awaken in another."

That is the message for you and Mom.

"When we die, we live."

67.
"I PROMISED DAD THAT WE WOULD NEVER PUT HIM IN A NURSING HOME. NOW I REALIZE IT WAS A MISTAKE TO SAY THAT."

It was easy to make such promises when Dad was in good health. When other members of the family passed away, they had short illnesses and the family was able to cope.

Now a new set of circumstances has appeared. Dad has been sick for months and family members who have cared for him are at the end of their rope. Either he must be put into a nursing home, or the health of others will fail.

The time has come to lovingly say, "Dad, it was a mistake to make that promise, but we still love you. We're going to put you in the best possible place and remember, you will be just as important to us as ever."

You will show your love for Dad in the selection of a nursing home. It is the most important shopping you will ever do. You will need to decide whether he needs intermediate or skilled care. Intermediate care is for persons who cannot live alone but do not need constant medical assistance. Skilled care is for those who need professional medical care at all times.

As you visit nursing homes, think of things like these:

Are the meals served with taste?

Are the attendants friendly?

Are there enough activities and diversions to keep residents interested?

Does the staff exhibit a caring attitude?

Are there provisions for privacy?

Do the residents seem to be treated with dignity?

Is the home close enough for the family to visit?

Do the residents appear happy?

Do some residents seem overdrugged?

Can your loved one take a few things to remind him of home?

Include Dad in the decision making. Let him know that his opinion is important.

When the time comes for him to enter the home, give Dad lots of attention — frequent visits and phone calls. If possible, invite him home often for a meal.

Let him know that your loving relationship with him has not changed.

Some older people find that the transition to a nursing home is a happy event. They are no longer isolated, they feel safe. An activities director encourages them to engage in fulfilling activities. And often the relationship between family members and the resident improves.

That brings us to the matter of promises. Does the Bible have anything to say about that subject? There is a strange story in the 11th chapter of Judges about a man named

Jephthah, who is described as a man of mighty valor. Jephthah was devoted to the Lord. When he went to fight the Ammonites, he made a promise that if he returned victorious, the first thing that came out of the door of his house would be sacrificed to the Lord.

Jephthah did gain a great victory, but he was dismayed when he saw his beloved daughter, his only child, come through the door. He felt that he must keep the promise and she agreed. She asked only that she might roam the hills for two months and weep with her friends because she would never bear a child.

There is some question as to whether Jephthah killed his daughter or whether he consecrated her to perpetual virginity.

At any rate, this strange story teaches us two things.

One is to be careful about the promises we make.

The second is that some promises should be broken. We must sometimes say, "I was wrong, I shouldn't have promised that. I'm sorry."

68.
"THE OTHER DAY I WAS THINKING ABOUT SOME OF THE PEOPLE WHO HAD MADE A DIFFERENCE IN MY LIFE. I WISH I COULD THANK THEM."

In reflecting on important events during his childhood, a Christian physician remembered that as a lad he had visited a church where he had participated in an evangelical service. It was quite unlike the more sedate services he usually attended. When the minister gave an altar call, the young man was too shy to leave his seat. However, he did ask Jesus to come into his heart, and he sensed a change in his life that night.

Years later, during a time of meditation, the physician

135

felt led to visit the minister to whose invitation he had responded. He met a discouraged old man who was surprised to learn that his sermons had been remembered and used of God to change lives.

This Christian doctor said that it was as though I had given him a priceless gift.

The apostle Paul was generous in giving out such gifts. In reading the book of Romans, one is tempted to skip chapter 16 which contains a list of hard-to-pronounce names of people to whom Paul sent greetings. There are more than two dozen persons, all of whom had contributed to Paul's ministry. Some had risked their lives for him. One example from verse 13: "Greet Rufus, chosen in the Lord, and his mother, who has been a mother to me, too."

In the most profound theological study in the Bible, Paul took time and space to thank the people who had made a difference in his life.

It would be a great spiritual exercise to write down the names of people who have had a positive influence in our lives. What did they do for us? How did they do it? Then we can thank God for them and, if they are still around, we can express our appreciation to them with a letter or a phone call.

For some of them, that will be a priceless gift.

69.
"SOME OF MY FRIENDS HAVE INVITED ME TO SPEND TIME IN THEIR HOMES. BUT I FEEL AS THOUGH I DON'T WANT TO BOTHER THEM."

With some planning and forethought your visit can bring happiness to your hosts. Think of your visit in these ways:

As you prepare for a visit to a family or a single person,

think about what time of the week would be best.

What are the circumstance of the family? Does the husband, wife, or both work outside the home?

How long should you stay? It can be too long or too short. Arriving in the evening and leaving the next morning is not long enough. Such a short visit gives the impression that you are using your host's home as a motel.

If you arrive in the evening, then spend a full day and leave the next morning, you will have a chance for good fellowship without wearing out your welcome. In some cases, two full days and three nights might be appropriate. Staying longer may be a burden.

An old saying puts it well, "Fish and guests stink after the third day."

If our arrival time is in the evening, my wife and I tell our hosts that we will have eaten before we arrive — there's no need to prepare a meal for us. That relieves the pressure on both of us — no fuming for our hosts if we are late, no nail biting for us if we are delayed in traffic jams.

And speaking of meals, we suggest that we would like to take our hosts to eat in a restaurant at least once during our stay. Your conversations with your hosts can make the visit a precious time for them and for you. It will be a time of sharing some past experiences. Think of ways your friends have made a contribution to your life.

On one trip we visited briefly with two couples we had known in a church years before. This was a chance to tell them how much their service had meant. Their work had not been forgotten.

Your visit will be a time to listen to what's been happening in your friends' lives and, perhaps, to hear some of their problems. Many people welcome the chance to share concerns with somebody not currently involved in their lives. If there is a problem, the couple may have already talked it into the ground. They need someone else to listen.

As you listen, think of these things:

Give the person an opportunity to talk without immediately chiming in with an experience of your own.

In your part of the conversation, repeat some of the things the other person said. "You mean...." and then say it the way you heard it.

Ask for more details to fill out the picture.

Maintain eye contact and look interested.

At an appropriate time, you may share a similar experience or give some advice.

Such conversations are golden opportunities to make a difference in people's lives. A psychiatrist once said, "If people had friends, we'd be out of business."

A visit is a great time to learn. My wife and I have never visited a home without learning something new. Some examples:

How a grandmother continues a lively correspondence with grandchildren hundreds of miles away.

How a family developed a puppet ministry in their church.

How a man carried on a scavenger hobby with an electronic metal detector.

Your visit will be a happy one if you blend in with the family. If you are there on Sunday, go with your hosts to church. You may find ideas you can take back to your church.

On one visit, I accompanied a friend to a Saturday morning breakfast meeting where I met several men doing interesting things.

More contacts, more new ideas, more enriching experiences.

When you leave, thank your friends and say something good about your time together. When you return home, write a note thanking them again for their hospitality with, perhaps, an invitation to visit you. Write about some of the fun things they could look forward to doing when they come to your home.

My wife recalls happy experiences with friends by taking a picture of our hosts and sending them a print in a Christmas card. It's a way of saying, "We had a happy time together. Let's make it happen again."

Motels and restaurants are the same everywhere. But friends are different. Each one is a special gift from God.

You may be God's messenger, chosen to bring joy into your friend's life.

70.
"I FIND IT HARD TO KEEP CONNECTED WITH MY FRIENDS."

Here's one way that my wife and I have found to do that. We gather up the Christmas cards and Christmas letters we receive each year and use them as a part of our devotional time each morning.

These cards and letters arrive, several at a time, during the busy Christmas season. They are read hastily, and we really don't digest everything in them. Now, on different days throughout the year, we take a few minutes to think about one or two persons who sent us a greeting card or letter. We put what they have written together with other things we know about them and pray that God will touch their lives.

There is no better way to keep connected with others than to pray for them.

When we take time to reread the letters carefully, we are often inspired.

Some of the cards have beautiful, meaningful messages. One that we received last year said, "How wonderful it is to know that our hope is not based on what we can do for God but on what Christ has done for us. How deep is His peace...how great is His love!"

One friend of ours shared words in his letter that his wife wrote before she died of cancer. "I don't know whether my remaining time is measured in days, months or years; but I am grateful for each day God gives to me to share with you." Those are words for us all. Each day is a gift, each is a treasure.

We understood the needs of a woman who wrote, "My daughter lives up north, but I never hear from her. I do a lot of praying and I know these prayers will be answered."

I was moved by the simple statement one of our friends wrote about the death of her husband, "Bob left to go to heaven, October 30."

Sometimes people tell us about trips they took during the year. It makes us say, "That sounds like fun, maybe we should try that." Some people invite us to come see them. We think about taking them up on it.

One man with whom we had worked wrote, "These annual letters bring back wonderful memories of shared service in the sixties." That made us think of those years.

For years one couple has sent a gospel tract in their Christmas card. The husband, retired from an executive position in a large company, wants to witness to his friends at Christmas time. We ask ourselves, "Are we making the most of the opportunities of this season to share our faith?"

A missionary family who had just been evacuated from their station in Congo (formerly Zaire) wrote, "We believe that the safest place in the world for us is in the center of God's will, and we believe that is where we are right now."

One of our friends is now in a wheelchair from complications of a polio attack. His wife wrote that Hal teaches Sunday School and does interesting wood working projects. We are inspired when we hear from this couple.

As we pray for these folks, we thank the Lord for our association with them and for what they've added to our lives. We pray that God will meet their needs that day.

Reading that card or letter sometimes prompts the thought, "We should give them a call. We can tell them that we prayed for them this week and ask about what is going on in their lives."

A note from us during the middle of the year might mean more to our friend than it would at Christmas time.

For those with access to e-mail, short notes may be sent to people anywhere. A missionary would appreciate knowing that we had read her newsletter and prayed for her. I might even ask her to return an e-mail message sharing something about the work that we could tell our Sunday school class.

Prayer keeps us connected with our friends. All of us can pray. A comment on one of our cards reminds us, "Friends may be the most important earthly wealth we can accumulate."

71.
"MY FRIEND JUST DISCOVERED THAT HER SON IS GAY. I WAS DUMFOUNDED, I DIDN'T KNOW WHAT TO SAY TO HER."

For many families, that discovery is a disaster — akin to finding that a family member has cancer or learning that he has been arrested for a crime.

Let us think about Christian teaching on the subject and then about what our attitude should be toward a homosexual person.

The Bible condemns the practice of homosexuality. The clearest passages on the subject are Romans 1:24-27 and Leviticus 20:13. A majority of Christians do not accept homosexual behavior as a valid lifestyle. One mainline Protestant denomination passed the following resolution: "The practice of homosexuality is incompatible with Christian teaching."

But we need to distinguish between homosexual practice and homosexual orientation. Usually, people do not choose their sexual orientation and it is unclear how it comes about. For a long time it was supposed that poor parenting or role modeling caused a child to be gay. That is disputed now. Homosexuality may be learned from peers, or it may be inherited. It may come in more than one way.

People with both homosexual and heterosexual orientations can, and many do, remain celibate. The Bible condemns any kind of sexual relations outside of marriage between a man and a woman. Contrary to what our modern culture communicates, celibate people can live happy, fulfilled lives.

Some people with a homosexual orientation have, through prayer, counseling, and the help of a support group, come to the place where they can have a relationship with a person of the opposite sex, even if the homosexual tendencies are not completely erased. Activist homosexual groups ridicule this possibility, but it does happen.

Suppose we find that someone in our family is gay or lesbian, perhaps even practicing this sexual behavior. How should we react to this?

The heart of the matter is that we can love such a person without accepting the validity of the behavior. These are points to share with any parent concerned about this problem:

1. Parents should not condemn themselves. They may have had nothing to do with the sexual orientation of their child.

2. One's sexual orientation does not nullify the worth of a person. He still has gifts and talents. That person is loved by God and has value in His sight.

3. The homosexual child may be suffering more than we realize. Many homosexual people wish they could change and some have tried to do so without success.

4. Men and women with a different sexual orientation often worry about their relationships with family and friends. "Do you still love me? Can I still live here?" are thoughts that go through their minds.

5. If someone confides in you about his/her sexual orientation, listen and try to understand. Don't change the subject.

6. Respect the confidentiality of what is told to you. The person may not be completely out of the closet. He/she may not want friends and employers to know.

7. Keep such persons in the family, invite them to family events. Let such persons know that you care about them.

8. At the same time, you should not be pushed into saying that a gay lifestyle is fine, if you think it is wrong. There is enormous pressure from the world today to accept homosexual behavior as a valid, alternative lifestyle. If this comes up in a conversation, you have a right to state your conviction. Parents have the right to refuse to permit immorality in their homes from children of either sexual orientation.

We are to love righteousness and we are to love people.

"...and be ye holy: for I am the Lord your God" (Lev. 20:7 KJV).

"Beloved, if God so loved us, we ought also to love one another" (1 John 4:11 KJV).

It's hard sometimes to put the holiness and the love of God together. But they are together in the heart of God. And it is our goal to become godly men and women.

72.
"IT BOTHERS ME THAT I STILL RESENT SOME OF THE PEOPLE IN MY PAST."

Jesus described an unforgiving spirit as one of the greatest spiritual problems. Immediately after the Lord's prayer, Jesus said, "For if you forgive men when they sin against you, your heavenly Father will also forgive you. But if you do not forgive men their sins, your Father will not forgive your sins" (Matthew 6:14,15).

To put it another way, we can't have a good relationship with God when we have bad relationships with other people.

It's also impossible to be a healthy human being when we hate someone. One man put it this way, "The moment I start hating a man I become his slave. I can't enjoy anything I do because he is always in my thoughts. He hounds me wherever I go. When the waiter serves me steak and strawberry shortcake, it might as well be stale bread and water. My teeth chew the food, but the man I hate will not let me enjoy it."

A spiritual breakthrough comes when we ask forgiveness from God and initiate a reconciliation with the person we resent.

When you pray, first thank the Lord for the people you love. Then start praying for the person against whom you bear some resentment. Think of the verse, "...Love your enemies and pray for those who persecute you..." (Matthew 5:44).

Then name the person you resent and ask the Lord to bless his life. Pray that he will have a good day. Pray for his family.

If you feel that you're dishonest in praying this way, ask the Lord to change you. Follow that by repeating the prayer for the well-being of the man or woman you resent.

Next, in some way, let that individual know that you have forgiven him. If God had not taken the initiative, we would never have known of His forgiveness. "But God demonstrates his own love for us in this: While we were still sinners, Christ died for us" (Romans 5:8).

Your initiative may be a letter or a phone call. That could be a hard thing to do, because your overture may be rejected. It's more likely, though, that the other person will welcome the end of the estrangement.

One man wrote to a community where he felt that some resented him. The issue he mentioned was not remembered by anyone. No matter, he had done what he needed to do to free himself from the guilt he felt.

More than thirty years ago in a certain church, there was a disagreement that caused much bitterness. Some left the church. Recently one couple who remained in the church visited a woman who had left the church. She was then nearly 90 and lived in a retirement home. No mention was made of the dispute, the details of which had long since been forgotten. But that couple's visit said in a powerful way, "We want you to know that we love you."

Everybody felt better that day.

73.
"I THINK IT'S HARDER TO MAKE FRIENDS WHEN YOU ARE OLDER."

We can find new friends at any age. Others are looking for friends. When we take the initiative, they will respond. Why not set up a plan to invite people to eat in your home every week or every other week? Select a different couple or one or two single persons. A meal doesn't have to take a lot of work. For good fellowship, a simple meal is as good as an elaborate one.

Obviously, the people you invite should include some whom you really like to be with. But, every once in a while, add people who have been cool to you. You may find that they are really warm, friendly people. And, occasionally, invite a couple who are never likely to be invited out to eat.

My wife and I look for new people in church and invite

them to eat lunch with us Sunday noon. People don't find this hospitality in every church. They might come back.

When you find people who are not interested, don't be discouraged. They have their reasons. Just invite someone else.

In some churches, groups of people meet with each other for supper. In our church it is called Supper Eight. Three couples and two single persons meet four times for meals at different homes. We have come to know more people in this activity than in any other in the church. It might be an idea for your church.

A friend of mine told me about an 85-year-old woman who attends the meetings for international students in her church. She invites some of these young people to her home and shares her faith and other wisdom with them. She continues correspondence with many of them after they return to their countries.

How about contacting some friends with whom you have lost touch? Several years ago I sent a Christmas card to a couple saying that I would like to get together with them again. Immediately, they sent me their Christmas newsletter and a personal note. We've been closer friends ever since.

If you tutored a child who was having trouble in school, you would perform a wonderful service. You might also find a friend who would teach you something about his world. The same would be true if you taught conversational English to a new immigrant.

If you joined a small group for Bible study and prayer, you would soon have new friends. Such groups have been available for women for years, but now thousands of groups for men are appearing because of the Promise Keepers movement. You may not feel that you fit into the first group you try. Keep looking until you find one you like.

When participating in a small group, keep these suggestions in mind:

1. Listen more than you talk.

2. Be interested in other people and their concerns.

3. Think of encouraging, up-beat things to say.

Let us think about our friendships this way. Some of them are people we love to be with. We all need these friends. You meet others who are not as much fun. They may be lonely people. They will take more from you than you receive from them. God will bless you for ministering to these folks.

Yes, it is possible to make new friends at any age. The secret is found in Proverbs 18:24 (KJV), "A man that hath friends must show himself friendly."

74.
"WHEN FAMILY MEMBERS ASK ME FOR FINANCIAL AID, I FEEL GUILTY IF I REFUSE."

A son in his thirties could be called a perpetual student. His employment is erratic. He is always taking more academic work, seeking new degrees. He depends on his parents for some of his living expenses and tuition costs. The parents see their nest egg diminishing.

A nephew asks his aunt for $12,000 to help start a new business. He has failed in businesses before and returned only token amounts from loans received from family members. He is certain that this new business will succeed.

A granddaughter says that she will have to drop out of school unless her grandmother advances her money. Grandma knows that she could give her some of her savings and feels guilty if she doesn't do it.

There may be circumstances when we should respond positively to requests for financial help. If the need is genuine, and if we have the money, we may want to say, "Yes."

But responding to some of these requests may make elderly people "enablers" of continuing reckless behavior. Without money, the people who ask for help may have to make some hard, common sense decisions about their lives. For example, perhaps a person who has failed several times in operating a business should work for someone else.

Supporting a young person's education may be a worthwhile project. But if her grandmother doesn't help, the granddaughter can find other ways. Financial aid specialists at colleges say they can put together a financial package of grants, loans, and work-study activities that makes it possible for most students to pay for their education. Or, a student could stretch out the time for her education, do part-time work and pay her expenses.

We don't need to feel guilty if we have some savings. We have earned that, and we deserve the security. One little-emphasized point from Jesus' saying, "Love your neighbor as yourself" (Matthew 19:19) is that it is all right to love yourself. In fact, if we don't have some financial security, we will not be able to help anyone. The Good Samaritan could aid the roadside victim because he had a donkey, some supplies, and money enough to pay the man's bill at the inn.

When deciding about the distribution of our money, that is a matter between ourselves and the Lord. To plan well, here are some questions to ask:

Do I have enough savings to meet emergencies such as illness and possible nursing home care?

Am I being fair to my whole family? Some ask for money, but should I also think of those who do not ask?

We don't need to feel guilty about having a nest egg.

We should not let anyone pressure us into making a decision.

We have the right to refuse appeals from others.

We should think seriously about how God wants us to distribute our money, and act accordingly.

75.

"I HAVE SOME THINGS I WANT MY FAMILY TO REMEMBER WHEN I'M GONE. I WONDER ABOUT THE BEST WAY TO SAY THESE THINGS."

Several years before she died, my mother wrote a letter to my brother and me describing how she had prayed for us through the years. She told us of times when she sensed that God had been especially close to our family.

She reminded me of times when she felt that prayer had saved my life. She recalled her prayers for me during a time when I was applying for a scholarship to Columbia University, which seemed out of my reach, but which I eventually received.

I've reread that letter a number of times.

In prison and with an unknown future before him, the apostle Paul wrote some profound truths in his letter to the Philippians. That letter is also filled with warm personal references of appreciation and loving concern.

Several times in the first chapter he recalls beautiful experiences he had shared with them:

He said, "I thank my God every time I remember you" (v. 3).

He expressed appreciation for their concern for his needs during his missionary journeys (4:14-16).

He mentions people by name, sometimes expressing gratitude, sometimes gentle correction.

It is a love letter that still warms us.

For most people, a letter is the best means for communicating messages from our heart. It's often awkward to find the right time and place to say important things in person. Phone calls are good for keeping in touch, but not the best way to share messages that reveal our deepest emotions.

Consider the value of letters:

1. They provide the opportunity to choose your words carefully.

2. They can be read in private, but they may also be shared with others.

3. They may be reread many times.

4. They may be kept with family records, and perhaps passed on to other generations.

What do you want to say to your children or grandchildren?

That you love them?

That you appreciate what they have contributed to your life? Here might be the place to mention special experiences such as times you travelled together to exciting new places.

That you have traced the hand of God in their lives through the years? You might recall here some crisis where God seemed especially close to the family.

That you are praying for them? That you are dreaming of ways God is going to use their gifts and talents?

You could send this letter to your children years before you die, as my mother did. Or, you might place several copies of it with your will in a safety deposit box.

Do it while you still have energy and a clear mind.

A letter from your heart may be your most valuable legacy.

May we hear from you?

It is our hope and prayer that this book has helped you realize God's love in a greater measure and deal with some of the concerns of the 50+ years. We realize, however, that no book can cover every subject of interest to each reader.

If you have a special concern or concerns not covered in this book, we would like to hear from you. We hope to do a second book in the near future on similar subjects.

Please write your concern or question on the lines below, or on a separate piece of paper if you wish, and mail it to the address below.

_____

_____

_____

_____

_____

_____

_____

_____

Willard Scofield — 50+ Years
MAGNUS PRESS
P.O. Box 2666
Carlsbad, CA   92018

INDEX

Numbers refer to chapter numbers.

INDEX

Other Books to Enrich Your Life

What the Church Owes the Jew -
Leslie B. Flynn

Leslie Flynn's 40-year ministry to Jews qualifies him to share passionately of the Jewish contribution to the Church Jesus founded. He tells us why the Bible is essentially a Jewish book; why we owe the Church itself to Jews who risked their lives for Christ; that anti-semitism is senseless and ungodly; and how we can appreciate and love Jewish people. Foreword by Moishe Rosen, founder of Jews for Jesus.
ISBN 0-9654806-3-1   paper $12.00

Yes We Can Love One Another! *Catholics & Protestants Can Share A Common Faith* - *Warren Angel*

Christ's Church cannot be seen in disharmony and acrimony, for Jesus prayed that His disciples would be one in love. Evangelical minister Warren Angel shows us how Catholic and Protestant believers can love one another by under-standing their common bond in Jesus Christ, and by breaking down misconceptions and false barriers to fellowship and mission. Then, in love, we can be a Church of power and joy in the Holy Spirit. A book for all traditions!
ISBN 0-9654806-0-7   paper $12.00

Jesus in the Image of God
A Challenge to Christlikeness - *Leslie B. Flynn*

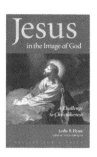

An antidote to the views of the Jesus Seminar! The real Jesus of the Gospels was a King among men who, though often abused and vilified, denied Himself to serve the poor, the sick, the sinful, and the outcast with a loving heart and healing ministry — God's own nature and likeness. Jesus still challenges us to become like Him. Can we do this? Should we even try? Leslie Flynn says *YES* and shows us how!
ISBN 0-9654806-1-5   paper $12.00

Available at Your Favorite Bookstore
or Call: 1-800-463-7818
Magnus Press, P.O. Box 2666, Carlsbad, CA 92018